# HUGGING S[illegible]

## A SELECTION OF POEMS 1995-2020

BY
TONY GOLDMAN

**Published by Easebourne Enterprises**
7 Hurst Park, Midhurst, West Sussex
GU29 0BP



First published 2020

Available from www.lulu.com/shop

ISBN 978-1-71667-805-9

For Anne

My greatest supporter
and harshest critic

# PREFACE

These poems have all appeared in one or other of my annual Slim Volumes (SVs) sent, unsolicited, to a few long-suffering friends and relations over some 25 years. I have been encouraged to maintain this tradition by the fact that none of the SVs has so far been sent back. Indeed it was a few kind recipients themselves who suggested that I should bring out a retrospective volume of Collected (or at least 'Selected') poems. The Slim Vols must, in spite of their slimness, have been taking up too much shelf space.

So here it is: between the covers of one book a selection comprising roughly one quarter of all the SV poems, those which seem to me in some sense worthy of this more prestigious packaging.

I should like to thank Philippa Martin, whose glass sculpture of Mozart's *Magic Flute* characters, Papageno and Papagena, was the basis of the cover design and the graphics at the start of each section. My thanks also to all those whose presence lurks within and among these pages, or who have been the inspiration for them. And my especial thanks to Jonathan Griffin, who speaks to computers on equal terms and who has been the midwife in bringing this volume into being.

Midhurst
July 2020

# CONTENTS

# PART 1 – POEMS 1995-1999

# DOGGEREL DREAMS

*In far Tibet there lives a lama,*
*He got no poppa, got no momma.*
*He got no wife, he got no chillun,*
*Got no use for penicillun.*
Ogden Nash

One accused of *writing doggerel*
Will huff and puff just like a jogger'll,
And from a modest rung of culture's ladder
Will serve up rhymes like Ogden's, only badder.

Or if his sobriquet is *versifier*
That's little better than a curse, if higher
Than that of *rhymester*, lowest of the low,
Damned with faint praise, just like an 'honest Joe'.

Maybe his skill, embracing loftier thoughts,
To offer more than craftsmanship purports,
Though critics cry: "If that be *poetry*
The Ark was fashioned from a Noah-tree!"

Yet one day he may get his crowning boost
To hear folk offer, when he's introduced,
That highest accolade - though few bestow it -
"I'd like you to meet So-and-so, the *Poet*."

# AUTUMN IN QUEBEC

The horseshoe heights round Hudson Bay
Describe the great Canadian Shield
Whose old pre-Cambrian rocks obey
Its savage climate's will and yield
Deep clefts where glacial waters play
By forest canopy concealed.

To taste Quebec's September treat
We journeyed north from Montreal
All eager for the chance to greet
Her woods resplendent in the fall,
To slopes that wear at St. Jovite
The waning summer's coloured shawl.

Emerald, amber, copper, gold
And multifarious shades of red:
A patchwork quilt of tones untold,
An endless variegated bed
Whose transitory splendours hold
Until the cause of them are shed.

These patterns, never two the same,
Our thirst for beauty almost slake,
They lend an erubescent frame
To mountain, waterfall and lake
And render wilds that none can tame
A little gentler, less opaque.

But autumn has not long to last:
The morning harbours winter's bite,
Soon leaves will die and snow will cast
A shroud, as spectral colours might -
If through an anti-prism passed -
Dissolve together into white.

# WINTER WEDDING

*For Stephen and Lisa*

"When my best man and I
Standing at the front of the church
Turned round
And saw her approaching on her father's arm
We were gobsmacked
And I thought:
This is something else
It has to be the greatest moment of my life."
Thus our first-born at his wedding speech
With words so unaffected and sincere
We all but wept.
Later that evening
After the festivities
(The wide-eyed bridesmaid with her golden curls
Chasing the willing page-boy round the hall,
The dimpled cousins with their lethal smiles
Eyeing the talent on the disco floor)
The couple came out into the icy courtyard,
The moon sharp and brilliant
Against a clear black sky,
Lending the frozen fields and timbered barns
A silver bridal veil.
And after they had gone
We stood for a minute
Silent on this rare night in winter,
Eyes once more a little moist,
Not just for the cold
But, as great music to a receptive ear
Sharpens the consciousness,
Because we felt that nature
With a fond conspiracy
Had by its beauty sealed the sacrament
Of this momentous day.

## TIME-WARP

*The 1911 Solvay Conference was the first in an annual series convened in the Hotel Metropole in Brussels which provided a focus for the great debates of the early 20th century on physics and chemistry.*
*Sitting: Nernst, Brillouin, Solvay, Lorentz, Warburg, Perrin, Wien, Mme. Curie, Poincaré*
*Standing: Goldschmidt, Planck, Rubens, Sommerfeld, Lindemann, de Broglie, Knudsen, Hasenöhrl, Hostelet, Herzen, Jeans, Rutherford, Kamerlingh Onnes, Einstein, Langevin*

In central Brussels in the Place Brouckère
The Hotel Metropole still stands four-square,
A monument from eighteen ninety-four
To Alban Chambon's fabulous décor.
Commissioned by the wealthy Wielemans
Even to-day its period grandeur stuns;
Pink Tunisian marble lines the halls,
Wrought-iron chandeliers light the walls
And here and there a gilded mirror offers

Reflections of the moulded ceiling-coffers,
While all around a Graeco-Roman frieze
Lends style the sternest connoisseur would please.
First quality, then fashion supervenes
And with it statesmen, artists, princes, queens
And many a mounted tribute there attests
A century of celebrated guests.

Among the hotel's relics, one would claim
To have acquired a very special fame:
Of Solvay's Physics Conference behold
A sepia photo eighty-five years old:
Two dozen brilliant minds who helped reverse
Our ignorance about the universe.

First, eager Madame Curie, sitting next
To Poincaré, both studying a text,
The latter clearly finding more attractive
A face so fair and brain so radio-active;
Then Rutherford, tall, debonair and breezy
And narrow-eyed Lorentz, quite Japanesy,
With balding and diminutive Max Planck,
His well-known constant safely in the bank;
And Jeans (Sir James), elusive as a quark
Clean-shaven like a younger Kenneth Clarke;
And Goldschmidt, Rubens, Knudsen, Warburg, Wien,
(Teutonic names monopolize the scene,
Though Perrin, Onnes, Langevin, de Broglie
Would reckon hegemony as unholy)
All sharing an obsession which compelled
Nernst and Lindemann and Somerfeld
And Herzen, Hostelet and Hasenöhrl
Their scientific standards to unfurl.
The men, so formal, strange, almost grotesque
Include young Einstein looking Chaplinesque,
Brooding on General Relativistic theories,
Whose year of publication getting near is;
And Brillouin, whose head seems half the size

Of Solvay's. What a gathering of the wise!
Surely the greatest aggregate IQ
Assembled in one photographic view.

Beyond the portals of the Metropole
Late twentieth-century Brussels bares its soul,
Reveals a restless, brisk Europolis -
To modern city-folk a living bliss;
Officials with conspiratorial air
Stride out to take their place at COREPER,
While chauffeured envoys speed along the streets
Bound for their mid-day gastronomic treats.

If from this busy square we were to peek
Inside the hotel, elegant and chic,
We'd see preserved as in some time-lord's cage
The guests, like ghosts from a more leisured age,
As if one world had by another passed
At first approaching, then receding fast
And by a theory now quite orthodox,
We'd note the slowing of the hotel clocks -
The march of time decelerated, just
As Albert Einstein told us that it must.

In the lobby where I pay my bill
The famous photo never fails to thrill
As, dazed by all that intellectual might,
I stagger out into the Brussels night.

## SIGHTSEEING

From the Villa San Michele in Fiesole
Florence lies across the valley, hazily,
Like a sunlit sediment seeping into the claws of the hills,
Guarding a hundred thousand cultural thrills.

Banks of purple bougainvillaea line the cool
Shaded path that winds up to the pool,
Lemon trees drop their fruit onto terraced lawns
And fountains play on cloven-footed fauns.

I picture the Masaccio frescoes at Santa Maria del Carmine
And Donatello's perfect sculptural harmony;
Shall I go and visit them, down there in the crowded city
And stand in hot queues? That would be a pity.

I think I shall stay up here, a glass of Orvieto at my side
And read about them in my tourist guide.

## Left Bank

My refuge in the *rue Jacob*
Is spared the general tourist mob,
A haven small and *sympathique*,
Much cherished by a loyal clique,
It sets our hearts a-throb.

Beyond the cosy vestibule
Its secret garden is a pool
Of quietude. While summer's sheath
Enfolds the street, the shade beneath
The chestnut trees is cool.

My private quarters are a pure
*Divertissement* in miniature,
A tiny, comfortable place
Whose bed is more than half its space
And much of its allure.

Upon the walls a silken sheen
Of damask cloth in red and green
And floral drapes above the bed
Have guarded many a newly-wed
And many a joy have seen;

While through the window at my desk,
Incongruously Romanesque,
Beyond old roofs of weathered grey
The tower of *Saint-Germain-des-Près*
Stands proud and picturesque.

Forget the Bristol! Shun the Ritz!
And philistines and thimblewits
Who rate the ultimate in style
A thousand-bedded concrete pile,
All garishness and glitz;

For here within this *quartier*
The *Hôtel des Marronniers*
Remains, however far I roam,
My spiritual home-from-home
And where I love to stay.

# Poetry Evening

*To Richard and Liz Woodhouse*

“Thursday being National Poetry Day
Come and dine and bring two poems each.”
And so we did
Bearing thumbed anthologies marked with yellow stickers
Some clutching typed sheets in italic font
Hot off the word-processor
While our host settled our performing nerves
With gewürztraminer out of large glasses.

First went the schoolmaster
Who read us some *‘Crow’* by the Poet Laureate
Telling of death in a difficult poem of hope
And having finished
Without a pause offered us an exegesis
So that no-one was quite sure
Where the poetry ended and the commentary began.

The barrister then rendered *‘Ode to Autumn’*
Reminding us it was indeed October
And therefore not inapt
And when he had done we all marvelled
At the sheer language, like the apples
Suspended from *mossed cottage trees*
Sounding like a first crunch into a ripe Cox.

Who’s next? The lady in the corner blushed
And gave a modern parody on *‘Hallelujah’*
With some uneasiness since, she claimed,
She was a non-believer.
It wasn’t so much the words, we were to understand,
She liked as how the poet
Had laid them out upon the page
In the format of a cross, but shame to say

The rest of us were scarcely listening
So eager were we all to take our turn.

Now the civil servant was prevailed upon
To read his poem. “It’s rather Grand”, he beamed
And told us of the swell
That sucked the stones on Matthew Arnold’s beach
Likening the ebb-tide to a loss of faith
(Avoiding the eye of the Hallelujah lady)
And then of a mysterious *darkling plain*
Where *ignorant armies clash by night.*
“Wow!”, we said and truly were impressed.

We took our meal and talked of poetry
What else? and who our favourite poets were
And can good poetry be humorous
And why is death more interesting than life,
Subjects rarely rehearsed in Reigate dining-rooms
Until we staggered forth replete with beaujolais
To face another round,
With loosened tongues and somewhat less control,
Of Sidney, Herbert, Hopkins, Larkin, Donne.

When everyone had had a second turn
And some were rooting in their cardboard folders
Eager for more
Our hostess rose. “Well that was nice”, she said
“Let’s save the others for another time.”
“I have a lovely one by Herrick”, someone said.
“Next time!”, we cried. The schoolmaster
Promising a composition of his own
Backed his car out of the gravel drive
Scrunching the stones like waves on Dover Beach
That day we came and brought two poems each.

# EASTER WEDDING

*For James and Sam*

As early Spring's pale, sleepy sun awakes
And warms the stones of Ramster's ancient walls,
It lures the birds that swoop across the lakes
To fill the gardens with their mating-calls.

The solemn rituals of the Registrar
Are lightened by a thousand Easter lilies;
How apt the faultless poetry-readings are,
How consummate the young musicians' skill is!

Above the evening's revelries we spy
The comet at its perihelion,
Spreading its tail as if across a sky
Confetti has been sprinkled freely on.

I marvel how it seems on every side
The omens tell of happiness and fun;
A fairy-godmother could not provide
A sweeter partner for a luckier son.

## The Laundry Tree

Early April and unseasonable heat.
We lay about the lawn
Already burning from the Spring drought.
Suddenly, 'Catch this!',
I threw back a fiendish one as if over the stumps.
Somehow, coltishly, he caught it
As he always did
And then we played Donkey which I lost,
But pretended that I'd won. It made him laugh,
As it always had.

I got the Pentax zoom,
Then saw the washing on the tree behind.
'I can't take that',
'Why not?', he said, 'Call it the Laundry Tree.'
And so I did,
(I have it here, untidy, ordinary, warm
As only family photos can be).
Later we laid the table
Exceptionally in the dining-room
With two large candles that I lit.
We touched upon the future,
But mostly joked and teased as families do
On such occasions like a million others,
But this one special.

Next morning you reversed the car
Stuffed with student clutter, for the last time
Down the drive and round the corner,
Waving and hooting.
I turned back into the empty house,
How empty! Yet how full
Of echoes and of bitter-sweetness!

# THE BATHERS AT ASNIERES

*Thoughts provoked by the Exhibition, 'Seurat and the Bathers' at the National Gallery, London, July - September, 1997.*

I have always had a problem with '*The Bathers'*
Whose admirers seem restricted to a few,
So I thank the National Gallery who gave us
The chance to re-examine it anew.

In the Salon where the work was first exhibited
The assessors thought its future wasn't bright;
They remarked on its 'prismatic eccentricities'
And they hung it in the café out of sight.

In this monumental study of Parisians
At leisure by the Seine at Asnières
The men exhibit curious positions
In which no-one of the others is aware.

Now I know that I should marvel at the brushwork -
How the tiny dabs of colour have been smeared
With a "pointillist technique" to use the posh-talk,
But frankly I just find the picture weird;

For the central youth's too static and anonymous,
In his size a false perspective is displayed
And, facing the direction that this *bonhomme* is,
I don't see why his head is in the shade;

And beneath his arm the experts see a shadow
Whose shape is like the outline of the sails,
But this hardly makes the work a Leonardo,
For Art more than coincidence entails.

In another room a riverscape of Caillebotte
Simply glows with iridescence and élan;
By contrast Seurat's paintings show us why a lot
Of people say he's just an also-ran.

I am sorry to be critical of Seurat
As his fame among the *cognoscenti* grows,
But about which paintings likely to endure are
The public can be wiser than the pros.

## "DEAR SIR"

There are people who achieve a certain fame
By committing unimaginable crimes;
In comparison my only vice is tame,
It's the urge to get a letter in the Times.

We admire the rugged heroes who prepare
For the steepest and most terrifying climbs,
But although courageous few of them would dare
To articulate a letter to the Times.

Even clever mathematicians who with glee
Meet the challenge of the study of the primes
Find that numeracy cannot guarantee
That they'll get a letter published in the Times,

And the poets we can never reimburse
For their treasury of memorable rhymes,
But it's fruitless to pontificate in verse
If you're trying for a letter in the Times.

How I wish I had the talent to compose
Götterdämmerung, Otello, Peter Grimes,
But no music is a substitute for prose
As a basis for a letter to the Times.

In not one of these attainments I am skilled;
Never mind - for when the final tocsin chimes
At the Judgement Day I'll claim a life fulfilled,
For I've had a letter published in the Times!

# EIGHT THINGS I SHOULD LIKE TO HAVE BEEN

*To Dilys Wood, on reading her first published volume of poetry*

Pianist like Alfred Brendel,

Escort to Felicity Kendall,

University Professor,

Duchess of Argyll's confessor,

One who painted like Cézanne did,

Present when the *Eagle* landed,

In the shade with Amaryllis,

Poet half as good as Dilys.

## *ÉNARQUE*

When Pierre-Henri Gascon de Villèle -
Diminutive, bespectacled, urbane -
Enters the restaurant *Vivarois* in the Avenue Victor Hugo,
The staff are respectful to the point of obsequiousness
As befits a graduate of the *Grandes Ecoles*
At the peak of his career. Being his luncheon companion,
I too am accorded a certain deference
And conducted to a favoured alcove by the window.

We have come here to negotiate; but first
There are matters of more immediate concern:
The menu and the *carte des vins*
Which must be given the time and space they merit.
Without pretence or condescension on Pierre-Henri's part
He and the waiter have become, just for a moment,
Professional equals, even conspirators,
Absorbed in serious talk of flans and flavourings
And whether the wine should be decanted first.
The outcome of this grave exchange of views
Is then conveyed to me in fluent,
If heavily inflected English.

Pierre-Henri tastes the Giscours `85,
Pronounces it acceptably mature,
Applies a fastidious napkin to his lips,
Enquires politely of my family,
Comments sympathetically on the tragedy at the *Pont de l'Alma*,
And finally
Invites me to describe Whitehall's position
Apropos the subject of our lunch.

I pull myself together,
Trying to ignore the vapours
Emanating from the *coussin de sole aux oeufs d'ablettes*
At the next-door table

And the eyes of Juliette Binoche
Pouting from a poster on the hoarding opposite
And the pale-green buds
Bursting on the plane trees in the avenue
And the *chic* Parisian ladies
Parading their spring fashions past the window,
And turn to concentrate upon his arguments.

'I quite agree with you', he lies, 'Alas,
The *Quai*, you know, are so unreasonable -
I could perhaps persuade them otherwise
If only I had your word that British Ministers
Would be prepared to meet us, say, half-way
Over our little problem in the Council'.
Aha! So linkage is their game!
What is the catch behind the emollient words?
But now the waiter is distracting me with the sweet-trolley,
Urging me to contemplate
The *feuillantine d'ananas à la citronnelle,*
Blunting my powers of ratiocination.
With a desperate intellectual lunge
I offer up a further compromise
And, *ad referendum* to our respective Ministers,
We strike a deal - and promptly celebrate
With armagnac*, hors d'âge*.

The bill, discreetly choreographed, is paid,
Likewise the courtesies of the *maître d'hôtel*
('How was your meal, *messieurs?'* - pure ritual:
He knows it was as near perfection
As human craft can reach). Our business over,
Pierre-Henri's thoughts are focussing elsewhere;
Politely he bids me a pleasant journey home
And, with a final *au revoir*, trots back
Towards his Ministry where he will soon
Devour the problems of the afternoon.

# FUTURE *SERIOSO*

When sex becomes a talking-point as commonplace as food
And vanished is the laughter it evokes;
When everywhere is openness and nothing can be crude,
What topics shall we turn to for our jokes?

When all that is described must be politically correct
Such as "cerebrally challenged" for the dim;
When gags about the Irish we are bidden to reject,
The outlook for comedians is grim.

Beware the day that pleasantries and puns become extinct,
When truth is always better than pretence,
When parody and humour with subversiveness are linked
And a smile becomes a capital offence.

# THE COUNCIL TIP

Some on Sundays not at church
Immerse themselves in other rites;
Before their morals you besmirch
Observe them at the rubbish sites

And contemplate a proud display
Of bonhomie, almost of fun,
As in the booths on Polling Day
When civic duty's duly done.

They travel there in shooting-brakes
Or small saloons with bulging boots,
With rusty beds and broken rakes
And grandpa's rancid pre-war suits.

Not for the squeamish or the soft
But T-shirt-men with tight-clad hips
Who hurl their bundles up aloft
And fill the Council's massive skips.

Each object: gaudy, dull or kitsch
Is bid farewell with scarce a tear;
The rejects of the poor and rich
Converge their various histories here,

While in the corners of the yards
Re-cyclable discarded goods
Are earmarked by the watchful guards
To supplement their livelihoods.

This casting-off acquires the spice
Of ritual: with fraternal nods
They make collective sacrifice
To stern environmental gods.

Say not these folk have gone astray,
Their faith than yours is no less keen;
For though forgoing Matins, they
Have to a burial service been.

## AUTUMN DEBUT

*To Natasha Goldman, born 8th November 1998*

It seemed appropriate
Your entrance should have been about the fall,
So warm and calm and colourful the scenery
To welcome you on stage.

High on the ridge
The bonfire lit a beacon to your birth
And rockets bursting over the Lammas Lands
Proclaimed your festival.

Of course the hillsides
Decked in yellow, amber, gold, vermilion
Were beautiful - yet were I a leaf
And saw you sleeping in your cradle there
I'd hold to green for jealousy,
Knowing of an even greater beauty:
One that shall survive a hundred falls
And still not fade.

# Red Tape

... enter high-street post-office clutching form
and join a zigzag queue between the ropes
a soothing automated female voice
says cashier number four please
move up and peer through plate-glass screen
at rubber stamps and piles of envelopes
and cashier number four
waiting for me and for her lunch-hour
can I help says she I clear my throat
I have come to declare sorn I say
an anxious look
she grips the counter ready for anything
what did you say says she
s-o-r-n sorn I say
statutory-off-the-road-notification
it's a new thing I say by way of explanation
just come out
car's not in use you don't pay tax
all you do is make this declaration
says so on the form
thought you said declare *war* says she
first one of these we've had
what will they think of next and stamps the form
I waltz out into the street
elated legitimised fulfilled
resolving to append to my cv
'the first person in Godalming to have declared sorn'...

## TEN CHARACTERS IN MAY

The Minister has always had
A problem with the spoken word;
He drives his civil servants mad
While fêted by the common herd.

The stewardess is keen to find
A passenger with whom to flirt
And chatting up the man behind
She spills the coffee down my shirt.

My xenophobic driver, he
Has never been abroad, but speaks
Of plunging planes and how to flee
The Channel Tunnel if it leaks.

My gentle friend has all his life
Advanced the cause of heretics
While, unbeknown to him, his wife
Was in the pay of MI6.

The Danish beauty scarcely knows
Her latent powers to entice,
But modestly says, "I suppose
Men like to look at something nice."

The clothing magnate thinks aloud,
"My wealth and servants are the fruits
Of leadership - why not be proud
That half the city wear my suits?"

The hotel clerk I like to call
My secret psychotherapist;
She makes me feel that I am all
She ever wanted to assist.

Applaud the wise Jamaican judge!
The delegates are all at sea;
He saves the Treaty - who'd begrudge
His rendezvous with destiny?

The French ambassador can lend
To any group an unctuous tone;
He likes to greet me as, "My friend,
The well-known English francophone."

The pundit labours to imbue
With salient facts his faithful sheep;
He puts the case for EMU
And half the audience to sleep.

# Cavendish Square

There are six huge plane trees in the square
Or it may be seven it's difficult to know
Which one you started with

It is summer evening

I am not really interested in the girl
With the long blond hair on the bench opposite
But from time to time I look at her
To see if she is looking at me
Wondering why I am looking at her

She is reading a letter on thick yellow paper
And is very smartly dressed
In fashionable black and white

On the grassy bank
Two lovers are engaged in foreplay

Just by the blond girl there is a plinth
Surrounded by white roses and a box hedge
Perhaps it is a monument to Cavendish
I can't go up and peer at the inscription
Or she may get the wrong idea

What if I approached the girl
(In whom remember I'm not interested)
And said
'Shall we go over to the grassy bank
And tell each other exactly why
We both happen to be sitting at the same time
In the same part
Of the very same London square
A circumstance so extremely improbable
As to defy the laws of chance?'

Dusk is coming on
The girl gets up to go
She flashes me the briefest of smiles
(Or do I imagine it?)

I stay sitting under the six enormous plane trees
Or is it seven? - it’s difficult to tell.

# RETIREMENT DAY

I made the staff canteen just before closing-time
The summer heat had seeped into the basement
Mingling with the blasts of hot air escaping from the kitchens
And steam rising from the metal warming-trays
Causing the stolid Dutch girls on the serving-staff
To mop their faces as they went about their business
Wiping spilt ketchup from deserted tables
And calling to each other in harsh gutturals.
I took my tray and chose the last two chunks
Of Southern Chicken fried in fat-soaked breadcrumbs.

All morning I had been loading
The milestones of my working life into cardboard boxes.
Behind the glass partitions of the meeting rooms
My colleagues were keeping the Ship of State afloat
But seeing me pass by looked up acknowledging
My special call upon their sympathy.

I carried my tray
To the table where I always used to go
To barter gossip with like-minded souls
And poke some mild fun at Ministers
Prolonging the break with cups of watery coffee
(Once our eminent Chief Scientist
Holding forth with dazzling coffee-talk
Had flung his chair back histrionically
Apologizing that he had to dash
Bound for the South Pole).
Now the room was empty
Save for a young Executive Officer
With even younger wife and two small kids
Up to the office for a summer treat
And a sickly-looking lawyer
Furtively scanning a doubtful work of fiction.

Did you notice this morning
How different people tackle retirement talk?
Some are dammed almost before they start
Willing one a long and healthy life
Adjectives whose frightening opposites
Weigh like shrouds
Others simply wish one a time fulfilled
A formula more tactful and humane.

Now I am into the canteen's custard pudding
Trying not to taste it
But no-one here expects gastronomy
And I want this last memorial meal
To have the qualities our meals have always had
(Yes, I have eaten for my country with the best
At *Comme Chez Soi* and *Ledoyen*
At standard rates of Travel and Subsistence
Financed by nights in cheap hotels
But that is another story).

The glasses from the previous evening's party
Have all been washed and packed away
And the stapler and the wooden-handled paper-knife
Have gone into my black official brief-case
Fully depreciated over many years
And so legitimately mine
And the last important document
Has been added to the pile of papers
I cannot throw away.

This morning, sitting in my high-backed swivel-chair
I had this vision
That the accumulated knowledge of my working life
Had started to seep out of my head
Eddy round the ceiling of the room
And disappear through the open door
Like a genie out of a bottle.
Perhaps indeed I was already fading

Like Bilbo Baggins bearing the Sorcerer's ring
While more vigorous minds
Waited to assume the reins of office.

Struggling to grasp the day's significance
At last I got up from the luncheon table
Placed my tray upon the moving belt
Walked purposefully towards the exit
Hailing the Dutch girls with elaborate courtesy
(Enjoying the startled look upon their faces)
Took the lift up to the atrium
Swiped my pass for the last time through the barrier
Pushed my way through the revolving doors
And passed quietly out into the sunlit street.

## MINACK

A Thespian shrine with granite lined,
Sheer cliffs its massive altarpiece;
Where else in England would you find
A scene so redolent of Greece?

An Attic amphitheatre laid
On rugged coast-line justly famed,
Proud vision of Rowena Cade
Who bid the precipice be tamed.

Aegean-like the summer sea
Shines turquoise on its shell-white bed
While evening sunlight, glintingly,
Ignites the rocks at Logan Head.

Then comes the night, the spotlights glow
And time and place have vanished, save
The ceaseless murmur far below
As land greets each Atlantic wave.

# PART 2 – POEMS 2000-2004

## HUGGING STRANGERS

*For Peter Tunstall-Behrens*

Drizzle turned to sea-mist as the day wore on.
The coastal paths were alleys of mud
And the droplets oozing out of the cliffs in summertime
Had become waterfalls.

The way to the cove was lit by flaming torches,
Across the garden of the big house,
Down slippery stone steps,
Between clumps of dripping tamarisk,
Onto the beach.

In the days since Christmas
They had raised an altar to the dying century
And to appease the new.

An hour to go.

A light was put to the fuel-soaked bales of straw
At the heart of the bonfire,
Sending a tongue of gold to the very top
Just as the fog lifted
And we saw the glimmer of other beacons
Far along the coast.

Now the houses on the cliffs were emptying
And people came pouring down the steps
To share this turning of the calendar
In fellowship.

At thirty seconds to midnight
Our leader stands upon a rock
To welcome the New Year in:

*"And I said to the man who stood at the gate of the year:*
*'Give me a light*
*That I might tread safely into the unknown',*
*And he replied:*
*'Go out into the darkness*
*And put your hand into the hand of God*
*That shall be unto you better than light*
*And safer than a known way.' "*

On the stroke of twelve
An ancient powder-canon split the night apart
And we broke ranks, dancing and hugging strangers.

Then in a circle round the fire
Two hundred hands were joined in Auld Lang Syne
As a salvo of rockets burst upon the sky,
Lighting up this little edge of England;
And a few of the girls and the young men,
As if at some primeval cleansing rite,
Leapt naked into the high-water surf.

*

So when did the new Millennium begin for you?
Was it on the stroke of midnight,
When the champagne flowed?
Or was it perhaps a few hours afterwards,
When, into a cloudless sky, the sun,
Our own stupendous bonfire,
Peeped shyly over the Lizard ridge,
Flooding the bay with pale yellow light?
And would not that same sun,
For whom a thousand years
Is but one tick of its celestial clock,
Have smiled to itself to see our revelries,

Comparing our little milestones to its own –
The great eruptions of the universe,
The clash of nebulae
And the birth of new suns out of the cosmic depths?

# On Being Sixty

Defiantly we strode
The long, bare, western flank of Pen-y-fan,
Undeceived by the early spring sunshine
That lit the Beacons but left the cold untamed.
The highest ridge was lipped in snow
After the week's storms
And a grey-white film of frost on the northern face
Marked out our special mountain from the rest.

To each false summit we gave a name
To correspond with past reunions.
And so we called the first ridge *Twenty-one*,
Still green and confident of the way ahead.
Half way up we found ourselves at *Forty*,
Springboard to the arduous heights beyond,
From which the summit came again in view,
Masking the tracts of dead-ground in between.
Finally, the peak we christened *Sixty*,
Where every view was backwards, bright and clear,
And every way was down.

That evening at the long table, candle-lit,
We raised our glasses to the climb,
To hills that look so worthwhile from below
But vanish when you gain the highest point,
How, coming down, the things that you had missed
You now had time and wisdom to enjoy,
Like the stream
That races past the quoins at Brecon Bridge,
Born from a thousand silver strands
Out of the damp haunches of the mountainside.

## SEPTIC ISLE

If you're looking for an undemanding, restful place to stay,
There's an island off the coast of France they call *Noirmoutier*;
It doesn't boast much scenery – it's featureless and flat,
Has no cultural attractions – we can thank the Lord for that.

If stress is what you're used to and the mobile is your friend,
If the pace of modern living is the pace to which you tend,
Don't fret, forget the internet, develop other likes
As we both did in *Noirmoutier* the day we hired bikes.

If last you rode a bicycle some thirty years ago,
Then you've probably forgotten what you surely used to know:
That the saddle of this vehicle – the devil would agree –
Doesn't seem to suit the structure of a man's anatomy.

But what the mind cannot foresee the body never fears,
So we took our handsome bikes equipped with five *dérailleur* gears
And began our exploration of the island's level tracks
With a pleasant wind behind us pushing gently on our backs.

Despite the boring country and the pressure on our piles
We enjoyed this eco-friendly way of eating up the miles,
But when we turned against the wind our lungs began to burst
So, recalling the *dérailleur* gear, I slipped it into 'first'.

A crunching noise ensued – it didn't take me long to learn
That the pedals had lost contact with the wheels they're meant to turn
The briefest of inspections now revealed an awful scene:
The chain was wrapped round everything save what it should have been.

You'll know, if you've encountered a defunct *dérailleur* chain
Just why it is a bicycle mechanic's greatest pain:
After thirty minutes' labour there was nothing more to see
Than a total shift of oil from the bicycle to me.

*

With chain restored at last we pedalled on with scarce a halt
Passing endless flat potato-fields and marshes full of salt
And bungalows whose owners might have seen the sea and sky
If they hadn't been behind the dykes that keep the island dry,

When, tired and hot and dusty, but encouraged by our zeal,
We reached the island's capital, *Noirmoutier-en-l'Ile,*
Whose castle helped defend the isle in battles long ago,
Though why anyone would want it, it is difficult to know.

We gained the final bend at last to normal life rejoin
At the price of fifty francs and an excruciating groin,
But happy in the knowledge that by self-propulsion we
Had made our contribution to sustainability.

# Armageddon

And suddenly the wood stood back
Letting in the autumn sun
Where men were felling oaks and clearing scrub
To re-create an ancient waterway
Its gentle curve now etched across the glade

Along the banks
Proud clumps of pale pink Himalayan Balsam
While from its bed the reeds and bulrushes
Bore witness to the past and hope to those
Who would restore a lost route to the sea

Upon the hour a quietness fell
And the men froze where their work had led them
Like statues scattered in a magic place
Invaded by no breath of wind, no sound
Only the goldcrests in the topmost trees
Singing its beauty and its peacefulness

We mused upon our own small sad obeisance
And on the pointlessness of all such rituals
That dignify humanity and give it point
On silences that speak when words fall short
Or after music's dying cadences
And as the silence grew we strove to grasp
How the same God at once could oversee
These decent men about their modest work
In one small tranquil corner of the earth
And those who raped the towers in New York City
Snuffing out so many innocent lives
In hideous, senseless carnage.

# MUSIC TO DIE FOR

Mrs Greta Horowitz, hospitable, gregarious,
Aspired to help the brightest of her pupils on their way;
So when she thought them ready she was eager to have various
Supportive friends and neighbours round to come and hear them
play.

I welcomed Mrs Horowitz's gracious invitation,
Never willing to be absent at the launching of a star,
So a perfect summer evening saw me taking up my station
In a corner of her salon (not too distant from the bar).

Our hostess rose to say she'd had the Blüthner reconditioned
In honour of her protégé we shortly would acclaim
And whose very next engagement was a date to be auditioned
As the student of a pianist of legendary fame.

And now to give his rendering of Schubert, Brahms and Weber
There appeared our youthful maestro looking confident and proud;
"He's very handsome, isn't he?" opined my ancient neighbour,
A remark I'd not have minded if it hadn't been so loud.

Reading from his notes the artist told us what was vital
Like the age of the composer when each piece was first performed,
Which furthered our enjoyment of his overall recital:
We all felt rather privileged to be so well informed.

The audience, it must be said, were mostly aged gentlefolk,
The summer heat was drifting through the partly opened doors,
So some of us were detailed to administer a gentle poke
Whenever our enjoyment might be jeopardised by snores.

Outside upon the terrace were some lively water features
Which gurgled through the evening making something of a din;
Beyond them in the shrubbery were many feathered creatures –
It's astonishing how birdsong can get underneath your skin!

Someone had a smoker's cough but coped with sensitivity,
Conscious that his frequent paroxysms might offend;
If my view had been requested – I was quite prepared to give it – he
Could well have gone outside until the piece had reached its end.

If you've come across those gadgets used by people hard of hearing
You may know that certain frequencies will tend to set them off;
Well, a lady in the audience, in other ways endearing,
Was wearing one that whistled in response to every cough.

The interval – and time to view the smart herbaceous border
While our glasses were repeatedly replenished by the staff,
After which it proved a challenge to restore a sense of order
When the pianist resumed his seat to start the second half.

He hadn't reached the half-way point in Schubert's mighty
'Wanderer'
When from a nearby discothèque an awful noise arose,
At the sound of which our man, who of his talent was no squanderer,
Brought the whole recital prematurely to a close.

The applause at last subsided and I nobbled our musician;
I said I'd been impressed how very calm he had appeared,
But was he looking forward to his imminent audition?
"Well, after what I faced to-night there's nothing to be feared!"

## A Short Life Of Haydn

Papa Haydn

Went to Eisen-

Stadt to widen

His horizon

## Falling Scales

I

A meeting had been hastily convened
In the forked tree where the X-Club met.
I sensed conspiracy from the sly look of the girl
Who had drawn the short straw. "We have decided
You should no longer be the leader of the Club."
The delivery, having been rehearsed, was faultless;
It zapped me like a bullet to the stomach.
It would have helped
If I had known the concept of a *coup*,
Or thrown some word like *Judas* in her face,
But dredging up a false insouciance
Shrugged "OK if that is what you want",
But my wounded look must have revealed it all.

I ran home through the woods,
Trees revolving round the sky,
Stumbling over crevices of shame
And lurched in through the kitchen door.
Tears welled out.
My oak tree world had just come crashing down.

Mother struggled to make sense of it,
Did her best, said it wasn't important.
Well, it wasn't to her, but that was a mistake;
She might have said that's how the world behaves
And so we'd better come to terms with it,
Than sought to stem the tears with sophistry,
Even when an oak tree crushes your childhood.

II

It was a kind of clockwork jeep
Brought by my Dad from a toyshop called America
Just after the war
That raced across the floor, stopped short,
Reared onto its two back wheels,
Turned about,
And then the driver leapt up in his seat,
Saluted, and raced off again.

I took it to school to show it off.
Sweets were rationed and exotic toys like this
Just didn't exist.
A knot of children formed into a ring,
The bigger ones keeping the small ones back
And all gazed at the brightly-coloured jeep
Going through its miraculous routine,
When a boy called Trainer marched towards the toy
And stamped on it.

The crowd melted away.
For several days they all avoided me,
Martyrdom provoking too much guilt.

III

At the next school I started to do well,
But couldn't stand Art,
Nor the vast full-bosomed art mistress Miss White.
I sat at the front painting stick-men.
In the classroom there was much commotion,
With coarse remarks about the teacher's girth
While her back was turned.
Goaded beyond endurance, she spun round:
'Hands up those boys who would like to be doing French'.
Seeing a deliverance at hand
And having been taught that truth is rewarded in heaven,
My arm shot up. The silence was intense.

I looked around to count like-minded souls.
They sat there, faces blank, arms on their desks:
The hypocrites! The massive woman
Rushed at me and seized me by the collar,
Marched me down the corridor in front of her,
Stopped before the door of the master taking French,
Hurled it open and pushed me into the room.
'This boy has had the effrontery to say
He'd rather French with you than Art with me!'
She slammed the door and strode back down the passage.

The master taking French,
Not pleased by these unscheduled histrionics,
To his eternal credit welcomed me,
Sat me down,
And quietly resumed the lesson.

# BEYOND SCHUBERT

When Tatiana Kojevátova
At eight embarked upon the start of her
Career as Russian violin prodigy
She played as if she were a God, did she.

At seventeen her life is looking rosy:
She's featured on a disc, 'Young Virtuosi',
Has just seduced the critics in Gstaad
And won the competition there – not baad!

*

Rehearsal time in Haslemere's bleak Hall:
To Tats the afternoon began to pall;
She found it difficult to understand
Why she was here with our provincial band.

She played some Schubert, trod on holy ground,
(Her Stradivarius made a pleasing sound)
She played it fine: just as her teacher'd taught her
And those who came were tickled by her hauteur.

Later at a party in the bar
With trepidation I approached our star;
"Congratulations, you were all the rage."
She shrugged, "I'm way past Schubert at my age!"

# RAMBLINGS FROM THE PEWS

In the presence of God…

For God is everywhere,
Even in the Registry Office
And luckily the Register
Turns up in every church.

*… and before this congregation…*

We've come here in our best to honour you
And maybe to show off a little too.
Just because this is a holy place
Cannot the air be charged with a little human frailty?
Though this time there can be no competition
Before the drop-dead Botticelli bridesmaids,
The ushers in their uniforms to die for
And the bride, with her lethal dimples, in soft silk.

*... forsaking all others…be faithful…as long as you both shall live …*

"I will!"
A huge moment, if you mean it;
You know that half this congregation over forty
Are on their second marriages at least?
If you really mean it
Shall we discuss it afterwards?
To see how you'll succeed where others fail
Instead of swapping stories of our grandchildren
Over the Sainsbury's sparkling chardonnay?

*... With my body I thee worship…*

A bit near the bone, this.
Does the Church really insist
This form of 'worship' be legitimised

Only through the offices of the marriage ritual?
Do they, hell.
But what would they prefer?
In an ideal world, I mean?
Each to his conscience I expect they'd say;
This is Church of England after all.

*... and by the giving and receiving of rings...*

Aunt Henrietta, near the back,
Dabs her eyes with a lace handkerchief
Soaked in Calvin Klein '*Seduction'*.
None of her fingers are devoid of rings,
Although for some of them
She now forgets the donors,
Except the fact that they were rather rich.

*... I therefore proclaim that they are man and wife...*

Oh! Do we have to clap
And prick the bubble of these high-flown sentiments?
This proclamation is a mountaintop
The human spirit rarely has to climb.
Please can we savour it a little longer?

*... Those whom God has joined together...*

This is where I try to pray.
You can't live all your life on such a plateau,
Talking of being forever true;
So how will both of you decide
Whether each step you take
Nurtures the marriage vows or injures them?
Suppose you fall in love with someone else
(And would the world not be a poorer place
Without its Tristans and Isoldes?)
Absent the pain where is the poetry?
Absent the darkness how will you know the light?

Morality would be devoid of meaning
If its antithesis became extinct,
Nor is it satisfactory
To clutter the antechambers of your mind with false piety
But let your demeanour be a spin-off from your faith,
As we should always do
When judging you.

*... let no man put asunder.*

So go your way.
To-day you are loving, serious, responsible,
Impressive like most young people nowadays,
And afterwards we will not speak of vows,
Or of the mountaintop,
But urge you an occasional review
As we ourselves might on our golden wedding day
Review the past
And draw the ragged threads of life together
Into a new-woven tapestry.

## Bird-Watching

Somewhere on the edge of Bassenthwaite
The ospreys have appeared to breed again,
Where troupes of Lakeland ornithologists
Are homing in to occupy the hides
With bottled water and binoculars.
The osprey!
Who, says Pliny, hovers high above,
Then diving down with great rapidity
Thrusts aside the water with its body
To seize its prey. Across the lake
They've built a wooden ledge up in the pines,
Lodging for the precious visitors,
And a hairy man with anecdotes to match
Claims to have seen their mating ritual
And has his story in the Keswick Chronicle.
All the while, oblivious of the fuss,
The birds play to a packed house, free of charge,
Though none would put a price upon their act.

*

There is a planet circling Betelgeuse
Where those who specialise in human studies
Can point their space ships towards planet Earth
And leap across the light-years in between.
Manoeuvring until geo-stationary,
They activate their non-detection shields
And, focussing their long-range cyberscopes,
Home in upon a favourite habitat
Where little knots of humans can be seen
Decked out in their blue-and-orange plumage,
Making their measured way across the fells
With object not yet clarified by science;
And sometimes in the season they call spring,
A pair engaged in mating ritual

Can be discerned in some secluded spot,
Which rare sight the Betelgeusians
Can beam across the inter-stellar space
To titillate a cosmic audience.

## Summit Rape

When in France they desecrate their landscape
In the interests of advanced technology
They do it with such self-confident *sang-froid*
Such bold *insouciance*
That you and I
Lost in wonder and in gratitude
Are led to feel that the amenity
Far from spoilt has actually been enhanced

On the summit of the *Grand Ballon*
Loftiest peak in all Alsace-Lorraine
From where on certain days you can see the Alps
A thin white jagged strip
Two hundred miles away
A massive trapezoidal plinth has been erected
Surmounted by a polyhedral egg

It is a radar station - and not a pretty sight

To appease the populace
A viewing platform has been built around it
Giving the direction and how far to anywhere
Etched in bronze with attributions
To the chiefs of all the myriad concerns
National, departmental, regional, parochial
Who planned and schemed to bring this thing about

But the masterstroke
And testament to the deviousness of the authorities
Is a sort of grand triumphal way
Up which the public proudly can process
From stony mountain path to viewing platform
A bridge to their Valhalla in the sky

Once aloft you cannot see the egg
For you are underneath it
Nor the vast unprepossessing plinth
For you are cantilevered out beyond it
What draws you is the stunning panorama
And the seductive *table d'orientation*
That makes this point a hub of Gallic pride
Linked by spokes in arrow-like trajectories
To Strasbourg, Nancy, Lunéville, Mont Blanc

Thus do the ruling classes condescend
And make a would-be thing-of-hate a friend.

# TWENTY-SIX NICE WORDS

Let *aposiopesis* be
To *baby* on its nanny's knee
A *cobweb* to engulf the mind
*Diaphanous* shroud that leaves behind
An *eleemosynary* thought
That *folklore* be more fully taught
As when *Galadriel* on her plinth
Bedecked in rose and *hyacinth*
Stood *iridescent* in the moon
(An image just a jot *jejune*)
And *kittiwakes* flew in to see
*Lugubrious* Melpomene
*Murmuring* lays 'neath tragic skies
That even *numbskulls* recognize
In *orotundity* of word
Like *plangent* cry of mockingbird
Whose *quiddity* will never break
The *rodomontade* of a sheik
And thespian *soliloquy*
All *tintinnabulatory*
Is voiced though *uvulas* to bleat
The oaths of *Visigoths* on heat
While *waterfalls* engulfing trees
Like justice forged by *Ximenes*
Compel the *yachtsman* to construe
This logodaedalistic *zoo*.

## Snowdrops At Ovington

Do you suppose the snowdrop knows
That February sun can never warm
When the air is silver-blue
And ice forms at the water's edge?
So is their name because they *look* like snow
Amassed in drifts
Along the wooded banks above the Itchen
Or that they fear not snow to flower?

Last autumn's rains
Engorge the river to a swirling torrent
Riding its channels under bare branches
Slipping clear over clean pebbles
Waterweeds splayed out along the bed
Like Aphrodite's tresses in the wind

And still where tortured willow roots
Claw their way along the riverbank
A tapering trail of snow-white blooms persists
As if some glacial god
Had fathered rivulets of ice
Flowing from their source at Ovington
To vanish in the warmer zones downstream

# TEASING GEORGIA

*In praise of yellow*

Through morning mist a wildflower vista,
Tufted Loosestrife, Tormentil,
Meadow Buttercup, Genista,
Oxlip, Cowslip, Tansy, Dill.

Larder-lust: a dish of custard,
Mango-flesh and treacle tart,
Honey-roast and fresh-made mustard,
Soft-boiled egg with golden heart.

*Teasing Georgia*'s like the Borgias:
Slaying rivals, turning heads;
English Rose, seductive, gorgeous,
Sporting in the nation's beds.

Sandy beaches, bottled peaches,
Topaz on a finger worn,
Faded leaves of calf-bound speeches,
Sunshine on a field of corn.

## HEATWAVE

The wood entombs its sullen spaces
Like a vast cathedral
Chestnut trunks its fluted columns
Canopy its vault
With living liernes of leaves

But here no coolness born of stone
These different
Shadows cannot keep the heat at bay

What grew upon the forest floor
Has withered, fire
Lurks behind the woodman's pile

And all so still
Our heartbeats fill the silence

Far away
Down a long dark tunnel
The cries of children on a sunlit beach.

# REQUIEM FOR A BIRD

*Concorde, 1969-2003, R.I.P.*

In flight, they say, it flexed
Like a fly-fishing rod,
Fly-by-wire by a finger's
Touch to a thoroughbred
Shaped to the air
And the earth's rim curved in blue,
Hanging steady at eleven miles
Like fixed in ice.

*

*Free of the land*
*The captain put his foot down;*
*We cabin crew would peer around the curtain*
*To see if anyone proposed;*
*They used to do it just as we hit Mach 2,*
*I don't know why;*
*That's the sort of plane she was,*
*Like a party,*
*Wall-to-wall champagne,*
*Rock stars and businessmen*
*Squeezed into faded leather seats, cheering,*
*Six hundred yards a second*
*And there before you'd started!*

*

Alas, the shock waves
Rolling off her wings over ploughed fields
Crashed into the world's green consciousness;
Her figures fell apart

And fairest Helen of the Troposphere,
Now a kept woman with a loud voice,
Had to be put away.

*

And yet the image of her smile
Slicing through the sun-lit morning sky
Like a silver bird
Will never fade.

## EINSTEIN'S SECRET

Reporters at the hospital in Princeton,
Crowding round the nurse,
The only witness at the death of Einstein,
Were told the world's most famous physicist
Had spoken as he breathed his last.

"What did he say?" they panted, notebooks poised.

Perhaps he had revealed
How scientists could quantise gravity,
Dropped a hint how one might integrate
The fundamental forces of the universe,
Or even offered up a formula
For world peace.

"I fear I cannot help", the good nurse said,
"I don't speak German."

# THREE ST PETERSBURG VIGNETTES

I

When a thunderstorm dislodged the angel
On the gilded spire of St Peter and St Paul
That guards the tombs of all the Romanovs,
They sent for Peter Telushkin, mason and steeplejack,
(Money being tight for scaffolding)
To scale the spire with only a rope and hook.
After weeks of toil the job was done,
At which a grateful tsar
Awarded Telushkin five thousand roubles,
A fortune for a serf, and free vodka for life.

Alas, Telushkin only survived three months,
Poisoned by an excess of alcohol.

II

St Isaac's cathedral,
Proud and massive beneath its golden dome,
Walls adorned with fourteen kinds of marble,
Columns of malachite and lapis lazuli
Framing a precious iconostasis,
Holy place of pilgrimage and awe,
Became during the Soviet regime
A museum of atheism.

III

According to tradition,
The poet Sergei Yesenin
Slashed his wrists
And hanged himself

In the lobby of the Hotel Angleterre,
Leaving a poem
Written in his own blood.

More recently research has found, however,
That Trotsky wanted the poet beaten up
For trying to flee the country,
Those entrusted with the task
Killing him through an excess of zeal.

And he who wrote the poem, so it seems,
Was the commander of the All-Russian Extraordinary Commission
  for the Struggle Against Counter-Revolution, Speculation
  and Sabotage,
One by the name of Yakov Blumkin
And no mean poet himself.

# GRANDPAS KNOW BEST

*"Can we have the one about how it all started, Grandpapa?"*

Well, in the beginning
There was nothing
Neither earth nor heaven
A yawning gap there *was*
But grass nowhere
To the north and south of nothing
Lay regions of frost and fire
Niflheim and Muspelheim
The heat from Muspelheim
Melted some frost from Niflheim
And from the liquid drops
Sprang Ymer, the giant
There was also a cow, Audhumla

What did the cow feed on, grandpapa?

You ask too many questions, little one

But last night, grandpapa, you said
In the beginning
There was an explosion
And very soon
In the first twinkling of an eye
Little particles started rushing around
In a sort of soup
A hundred thousand million degrees hot
When it cooled down
The particles got together
In swirls of gas
Until the soup became all lumpy
Like porridge

And the lumps of porridge became stars and galaxies
And you and me

And why not, little one?

But, grandpapa, you never told me
What happened just after the bang
Before you could even blink
And anyway the night before
You said there never *was* a beginning
As old stuff rushes away
New stuff is always rushing in
To fill the gaps
Everything is the way it is
Because that is how it has always been

Which one do you like best, little one?

I like the cow one best, grandpapa

So do I, my child,
But now it's late
It's time you went to sleep

# MENS SANA

*'While cycling is a popular recreation for healthy and vigorous youth of both sexes and all ranks, it is not understood by numbers who have somewhat weak or feeble constitutions or have reached or passed middle age, suffering from some of the common complaints at that time of life; to whom cycling would prove a blessing, bringing with it renewed health and strength, if they but knew how to use it properly.'*

*'Cycling for Health' by Frank Bowden F.R.G.S., published 1913.*

Suppose you're of a delicate or feeble disposition,
A victim of the ailments that occur in middle age:
Sleeplessness, dyspepsia or chronic malnutrition,
Or simply just a tendency to fly into a rage,

Or if your veins are varicose, you suffer from anaemia,
You're flatulent or fat or melancholia endure,
A Doctor of Velocity who comes from academia
Advises you should try his revolutionary cure:

*Don't fester, get a bicycle,*
*A tandem or a tricycle,*
*Support your spinal column*
*On a saddle that you like;*
*Improve your circulation*
*Bid farewell to tribulation,*
*There's no need to be so solemn*
*Get a life and get a bike!*

A motion of your lower limbs that's steady, smooth and circular
Is wonderful for those who would their illnesses expunge,
And modest perspiration cannot render you tubercular
If afterwards you treat it with warm water and a sponge.

If cycling on an empty stomach doesn't disagree with you
A ride before the sun is up may earn you some applause;
But don't expect that I or Doctor Zimmerman will be with you:
We find too early bicycling light-headedness can cause.

*Don't fester, get a bicycle,*
*A tandem or a tricycle,*
*Enjoy our rural byways*
*From the comfort of a bike;*
*Follow my solution*
*To improve your constitution,*
*For then* your *ways will be* my *ways*
*Cycle anywhere you like!*

In tropic heat the English find the dust and dirt coagulate,
Their cheeks devoid of ruddiness get haggard, limp and pale;
Their glands are over-active and secretions fast accumulate,
Lowering their spirits till they're comatose and stale,

But riding in the morning, or just when it is darkening
Dispels this sickly feeling as they healthily perspire
And then those lucky souls who to the Doctor's words are harkening
Will find their livers mended and their faculties on fire.

*Don't fester, get a bicycle*
*A tandem or a tricycle,*
*Pursue this latest pastime*
*With a friend or with your wife;*
*So give yourself a tonic,*
*You don't have to be bionic,*
*But in slow time or in fast time*
*Get a bike and get a life!*

Fellows of discernment from the peerage to the peasantry
Who've given up their steeplechasing, badminton, or fives,
And fear that now their daily occupations are too sedentary
Find bicycling will add to the duration of their lives;

And though it is a challenge keeping warm a man’s extremities,
The dedicated rider who his winter cycling loves
The prospect of some bracing air will face without a tremor, `tis
His habit to repel the cold with knitted woollen gloves.

*Don’t fester get a bicycle,*
*A tandem or a tricycle,*
*You’re not too old to learn to ride*
*With succour from a friend;*
*So relish your departure*
*With your three-speed ‘Sturmey-Archer’*
*As you cultivate the yearn to ride*
*The roads that never end.*

# VISITING THE BARBER

Visiting the barber,
Rhythms of a life;
Six-weekly harbour,
Surrogate wife.

But for the ritual
What would I be?
Wanderings perpetual,
Rudderless at sea.

Welcome the cubby-hole,
Sweepings on the floor;
Farewell my other role
Once through the door.

Dream-world overall
Soon as I arrive;
Soothed by wall-to-wall
Radio Five.

Two lives on a map,
Diagram of Venn;
Not much overlap
Now as then.

But O, mister hairdresser,
Gentlest of guides,
Father confessor
More than 'short-back-and-sides',

Would that my mission
In a lifetime spent
Had as little ambition
And as much con*tent.*

# NATASHA'S DANCE

*With acknowledgments to Tolstoy and Orlando Figes*

After the day's hunting
Natasha Rostov enters the wooden hut
With flushed cheeks.
The servants bring pickled mushrooms,
Rye cakes with buttermilk
And sparkling mead.

The old man, the one she calls her uncle,
Takes down his balalaika from the shelf
And dusts it down.
Gently at first he teases out
The strange accelerating rhythm of a song,
Sounds that have reached across the endless steppes
From ancient Mongol hordes.

Natasha is stirred.
She throws the shawl from her bare shoulders,
Sets her arms akimbo,
Stamps her feet,
Strikes an attitude and starts to dance.

The housekeeper, Anisya Fyodorovna,
Wipes tears of wonder from her cheeks
While the serfs watch by the doorway,
Amused and curious,
Perhaps with other feelings too,
As the beautiful, slim countess,
Reared in silks and velvets,
Emancipated by the hunt, the mead
And the old man's furious tunes,
Now leaping and spinning like a soul possessed,

With whirling petticoats and smiling eyes,
Gives vent to what lies deep within herself
And in her ancestors
And every Russian woman.

## ***La Source***

*For Nick and Anna*

Through steep narrow banks
On the flower-strewn flanks
Of the loftiest *Puy*
In Auvergne, you can see
Two silvery threads
Engraving their beds,
Innocent, delicate,
Soon-to-be-weds.

One of these streams,
So modest, it seems
Too small for a name
Yet the '*Dore'* it became;
The other's the '*Dogne'*
And the point where they join
Is the birth of the river
They call the *Dordogne*.

And many a tourist,
Pragmatic or purist,
Throughout *Périgord*
Has never been sure
If the flavour that lingers
From drops on his fingers
Can trace its descent
From the *Dogne* or the *Dore.*

The *téléphérique*
Swings down from the peak,
Conveying the bikers
And skiers and hikers,
Yet all unaware
Of how near they are there

To the two little streams
And the secret they share:

The leaping and tumbling,
Foaming and fumbling,
Skipping and stumbling,
Ripple and roar;
Down they are racing,
The mountainside gracing,
At last they're embracing,
The *Dogne* and the *Dore*!

# PART 3 – POEMS 2005-2009

# Vintage Thoughts

*On my 65th birthday*

Lined with many a liquid jewel,
My subterranean hub,
The cellar, sombre, cobweb-cool,
Retreat, museum, pub.

I lay the claret down in youth,
Its foster-parent I,
At first it's tannic, raw, uncouth,
Ungainly, bottle-shy.

I nurse the wine through every stage,
From awkward adolescence
Until its rounded middle age
And silky, pale senescence.

My bottles, when they're feeling blue,
Rude Bacchus I invoke
To cheer them with a word or two,
A reassuring stroke.

I brush the cobwebs from their racks
And groom them like a wife,
Then leave them lying on their backs:
They crave the peaceful life.

Most earthly joys wine rates above,
Therein the paradox:
The corkscrew kills the thing you love,
A death the devil mocks

And crimson fluid in the glass
That awful question begs:
After its fleeting flavours pass
What price the dead men's dregs?[1]

Besides, I bought them long ago
To lighten fading years;
To drink them now admits you know
Life's short and so is theirs.

The miser's much misunderstood,
His arguments presume
Delay will maximise the good -
Beware what you consume!

And thus I've found it common sense,
Though sophistry it sounds,
To justify my temperence
On hedonistic grounds

Until to-day – time for a treat,
Enough of stern abstention,
Uncork the '82 Lafite,
And toast the Old Age Pension!

---

[1] 'Dead men' = 'empty bottles'

## TOTAL ECLIPSE

When the great shadow swept in from the west
And a slice of night slid from the firmament,
Dogs howled, birds fell silent,
And the sloe-worm, making for safety,
Froze on the cliff path.

But we, wise children of Copernicus,
Had marked the moment in our calendar
And sought each other in the long grass
In summer,
In an hour of stolen darkness.

# RED KITE

*For Ruth and Tim*

Here come the men with baskets
And soft Welsh cadences,
Spreading carrion along the tarn's edge,
Sending avian signals over the crags,
Across the great high reservoir of Nant-y-Moch
To the topmost ridges of Plynlimon.

The watchers bide their time,
Willing the empty sky to come alive
And bring the kites down to their feeding-ground.

Look up! Look over there!
Black dots over the crest, a gathering
From skyline entrances,
Assume corporeality
Like planets captured in a telescope.

The shapes grow wings, a tail,
Plumage of white and chestnut-red,
And the flight! Most free and graceful of all the raptors,
Swift and still,
Borne on invisible airs,
Wings held forward, arched and angled back,
A man's length tip to tip
And the forked tail flexed for a rudder.

Teasing, they circle the tarn,
Keeping their distance,
Swooping, then soaring back against the slopes.
Suddenly one drops and levels out,
Skimming the bank,
And like a fielder diving for a catch
Scoops up a morsel in its claws,

Heading off in one smooth seamless move
To its mountain fastnesses.

Forty or fifty birds now follow suit,
The vale a criss-cross of trajectories,
Streaks of red and white lit by the sun
Like day-time fireworks, on and on,
Until the food is gone.

All for free! The greatest show on earth!
And where’s the critic that shall know its worth?

# BECK'S BRIDGE

*For Harriet and with obeisance to Wordsworth*

The waters break
And sodden hillsides wring their skirts
Into a thousand rivulets,
Merging down Mosedale into Duddon
Where the stream slips shallow over warm stones.

A debutante, new off the fells,
But like a courtesan,
Scheming to assume a beauty spot
Down the valley where the land gives way
And cataracts shake the waters into spume
To hollow out a narrow gorge
Where the round-arched packhorse bridge was laid
On walls of rock.

The stream, now silent over deep clear pools,
Reflecting emeralds
From sun-spots imaged through the trees,
Patterning the grey stone bridge
With veins of yellow and green,
Becomes a cleansing-place,
A fell-god's swimming-pool,
That draws us in
To strike upstream against the flow,
Under the bridge, through dripping cliffs,
To the falls above.

It is a Lakeland beauty, unsurpassed,
Upon that inward eye forever cast!

## SUNFLOWERS

The wary villagers
know only what they see -
a face without a past

Does it do good works, this face?
will it organize an evening's bridge
or mend a dripping tap, dripping tap?

Don't mention honours -
what are they to us?
why honour a face without a history?

Ah, but let the face have a wife
and let the wife win a prize for sunflowers
at the village show

Now the face can be the wife's husband

One of *our* faces

One of us

## A Pasty For The Landlord

*For Michael Tunstall-Behrens*

While there is time
And while there is still time,
Sweep the shavings from the workroom bench
To make room for the unrolled document,
Re-charge the tarnished inkwell with black ink
And in a hand wrought in another age
Sign the deed drawn up so long ago
To smooth the passing-down!

This morning, having roamed the land -
Yours until the fateful signature,
Along rough tracks, through heavy gates,
Beating at tufts of ragwort in the fields
From force of habit,
Up the ridge to where the coastguard's hut
Defines your boundary,
Land that the law calls yours
But kept in trust for those who shall come after -
You strained your eyes to sea towards the Stone
Just visible above the lowest springs,
One-time signal for a boyhood dare
To outflank the tide
And wade the seal-hole to the secret pools.

Overhead the seagulls cry,
Etch their curves across the sky
Above the surf's unceasing lullaby.

A land you love
Yet vow to pledge your love must pass it down
While there is time
And while there is still time.

Little will change at first to outward eye,
The crumpled trousers belted with a string,
The threadbare shirt
With red cravat for Sunday visiting,
The weathered countenance lit by a smile
And hear the valveless horn on stormy days,
Riding the wind,
Reach into the corners of the cove.

Now other minds will order the estate
Yet seek your counsel while they can
And when at last
The slow cortège shall wind along the cliff
Will weep, but give thanks for a man
Who found profundity in simple things,
Knew of the land the wisdom that it brings,
A Cornish spirit borne on angel's wings.

# Summer School

West from York the land is undistinguished
Fields and hedges meld into a grey-green wash
As the little train slices through the heat
Sending an uncooling wind along the corridor
And the light that will not be vanquished
This torrid summer
Races behind storm clouds
Their linings charged with massive voltages
Soon to be dispersed in splinters of fire
Forcing great columns of air
Inwards like a malevolent spring
In howls of retribution.

Flash floods
Cleanse the streets of this once fashionable spa
Washing off baked pavements into inadequate culverts.

But I shall be dry in a place of music
Where the masters wait to be revivified
By eager bows drawn across well-tuned strings.

# Prodigy

*A recital featuring Joy Lisney, 13-year-old cellist, Hindhead Music Centre, 21 May 2006*

Pallid, substanceless,
A waif, this girl, a cardboard effigy,
Painted in blue-and-white for a dress
With honey-coloured, half-size cello
Pressed against her like a teddy-bear,
Bringing her back to scale.

Arms of tiny gauge,
Scarcely thicker than the bow;
How can this frail three-jointed set of rods
Come out with such a multitude of tones,
Of seamless melodies,
Or have the force
To rasp out Shostakovich like an angry wasp
Caught among the strings?

Technique holds no terrors.
Look at her shooting up the fingerboard
In a single lightning swoop that slips the eye,
Locating an elusive high harmonic
With calm exactitude.

We struggle to come to terms with such precociousness
(As some lesser species might admire the way we walk
Without a conscious application of our limbs)
And see a face expressionless, transfixed,
The faintest of smiles
Playing like a shadow over pursed lips,
Not of conceit,
But that the effect of what she does
So naturally can be so beautiful,

Not *look* at me, but rather *come* with me
Into a land of musical delights
Where the embodiments of time and space dissolve,
The awkward room, the clumsy chairs, the clock,
Even her beloved instrument
Giving voice to sounds that she already hears.

And then the music, unencumbered, is revealed
As those unflinching eyes
Focus somewhere out beyond the room,
Beyond the house and up into the skies
To where the composer waits with outstretched arms
To greet her.

## ATAHUALPA'S TALE

*With acknowledgments to Prescott's 'The Conquest of Peru'*

From the darkest of the tales
That Spanish chroniclers have told
The Inca Atahualpa's hails,
A tale of blood and lust for gold.

*

The Incas, offspring of the Sun,
Arose from Titicaca's womb,
A glorious dynasty they spun
A golden web from golden loom

And from the ‘navel of the world’,
The plain where holy Cuzco lay,
Beneath their blazoned flag unfurled
The greatest empire of the day.

The title to each firstborn passed
Till Huayna Capac issued forth
And ordered his dominions vast
Partitioned into south and north.

So Huascar, under princely wing,
Took Cusco, capital of old,
While Atahualpa ruled as king
At Quito, ruthless, proud and bold.

But Atahualpa, warped with greed,
Vowed his foe to overwhelm
And marching south at fearsome speed
Brought war and bloodshed to the realm.

From dawn till dusk the battle reached,
The ground was strewn with warriors slain,
Long afterwards their bones lay bleached,
With Huascar’s loss his brother’s gain.

So Atahualpa ruled as king
An empire once more unified,
But ere his reign had taken wing
A small dark threatening cloud was spied:

A trail of dust from galloping hooves
Across the vast Andean heights
Towards the Inca stronghold moves:
Pizarro with his acolytes!

Till on the Cajamarcan field,
Surrounded by the Indian horde
The Spanish envoys there appealed
That he, the Inca, meet their lord.

"And there my general will attend
Upon your grace this very eve";
"I'll visit when my fast does end",
So said the Inca, "Take your leave!"

Back sped the envoys to their camp,
Spoke fearfully of the Inca's might,
Their ardour spent, their spirits damp
And doubting to survive the night.

Pizarro, though, rejoiced and claimed
The arms of heaven were on their side;
He cried, "Our foe will soon be tamed"
And lit the embers of their pride:

"Before the sun has risen a
Deception will be put in train
To take the Inca prisoner
And all his servants shall be slain."

Then, fewer than two hundred strong,
Pizarro placed his forces where,
All hidden from the Inca throng,
They watched and waited round the square.

His silent troops he moved between:
"Fight bravely at whatever loss,
Fight for your country and your queen
To swell the empire of the Cross!"

They wait there poised like coiled springs,
Their lord his restless men placates,
When all at once a signal rings:
The Inca's army's at the gates!

Then forward the procession rolled.
The man-god entered unafraid
Borne on a massive throne of gold
With palanquin of rich brocade.

Behind five thousand of his host
The Inca halted, gave a shout:
"I fear no living thing nor ghost
So let the white man now come out!"

*

Pizarro's chaplain, tall and calm,
The plaza's ancient stones he trod,
To Atahualpa stretched his arm:
"I greet you in the name of God."

The angry monarch cursed his guest:
"You worship beings I despise,
For look, *my* god sets in the west
Each morning in the east to rise."

He seized the bible from the friar
And cast it down with bitter pledge:
"My army shall meet fire with fire,
Your shame shall be my privilege."

At this Pizarro gave the sign
And waved his white scarf in the air,
His men advanced in lethal line,
His horses raced across the square.

The Indians were blinded, stunned
By acrid smoke and sulphurous fumes,
In hundreds soon by muskets gunned,
The paving stones became their tombs.

And then the cavalry rode hard,
With naked swords they clove the air,
All exits to escape were barred
By piles of corpses lying there

And Atahualpa, now devoid
Of pride or hope, his spirit stilled,
His army totally destroyed
And not a single Spaniard killed,

Was held as hostage, guarded well
To keep his wretched kinsmen tame,
Yet on his clan still cast a spell
When they to pay him homage came.

The Inca pleaded to be freed
And pledged that, as a minimum,
To satisfy his captors' greed
He'd fill with gold his largest room.

So slaves were sent to where, *in situ*,
Gold was stored at Vilcabamba,
Lined the walls at Machu Picchu
High above the Urubamba.

*

Gold poured in and cruel Pizarro,
Dreaming of his fame abroad,
Looked towards a bright tomorrow
When to Spain he'd bring his hoard.

Yet all the while the captive king
Did pose a threat that pleased him not
And so he caused his troops to bring
False rumours of an Inca plot.

Treason charges soon were brought
By those on oath prepared to lie;
Though hard in his defence he fought
The Inca was condemned to die.

To burn now as a heretic
The Inca's of his fate's apprised,
But bowing to this Christian trick
The prince agrees to be baptised.

Then all this solemn rite attend,
In holy water dipped is he;
A sweeping sword, and so an end
To Inca, empire, dynasty.

*

Thus a future was denied
The Inca race of old Peru,
Sad victims of a genocide –
So many vanquished by so few

And thus the harsh Conquistadores,
Acting in their Saviour's name,
Made the cruellest of their stories
Spanish history's greatest shame.

## The Boy From Krakow

The trees, I swear it,
Grow tallest out of this low valley,
Straining over the North-East Hampshire scrubland
To the far Downs,
Their huge spent leaves gummed to the wet ground,
Smudging outlines and bringing disorder
To the garden border.

The blower wraps me in a veil of high-pitched noise,
Prising sodden leaves off the tarmac.
They don't stand a chance:
Got you, you curse of autumn!
Go join your clammy fellows
That I may pile ever higher
Your funeral pyre.

At first I miss the pallid Polish lad
Creeping up the drive with his flat bag,
Keeping a respectful distance
Until I should pause from my labours.
He thrusts at me his sales pitch typed in English
And from his bag he fetches
A bundle of sketches.

I am taken with the boy's initiative
But also discomposed,
Being asked for compassion and a tenner
When all-engrossed in battle with the leaves,
So I decline the offer of a work of art,
Though talent my young wanderer from Krakow
Has no lack of.

And later was it just my tetchiness
That gave me such regrets?
Ah no, what lingered was his pencilled mermaid,
Voluptuous, on a rock, with long fair hair
And so well done!
Come back, sad Polish artist, sketch-book driven:
All is forgiven!

## Why We Float

'If wholly or partly immersed in a fluid,
A body, no matter if sinful or chaste,
An upthrust enjoys, be it Stoic or Druid,
That equals the weight of the fluid displaced.'

When old Archimedes got home from the office
Jaded by geometry hour after hour
And too much moussaka and too many coffees
Then would he have simply got under the shower?

A notion ridiculous! One of his braininess
Doesn't want soap in his eyes as he laves,
But rather relief from his varicose-veininess
Soothed by the fluid whose upthrust he craves.

We *may* draw the line at becoming a streaker
Displaying our nakedness out on the path,
But quite understand that old thinker's "*Eureka!*"-
We too get our finest ideas in the bath.

So as you're caressed in your modern jacuzzi,
Floating in bubbles, your cares worn away,
Offer a prayer to that old Syracusi
Who showed us why bath-time's the best of the day.

# STONE CIRCLES

A mermaid sings at Zennor,
Her tresses flowing free;
Wild gardens at Boskenna
Tumble to the sea

And southward sleeps Lamorna
Below a wooded vale,
Its picture-postcard corner
Safe from the wildest gale,

Then north to where St Buryan
Keeps watch in storm or shower,
From Nanzijal to Veryan
No taller, prouder tower;

While eastward in an unkempt copse
The fougou of Boleigh;
Its granite top drips filtered drops
That fell from a Bronze Age sky.

*

Here's many a 'merry maiden'
In a circle of West Penwith
And each stone heavy-laden
With the pregnancy of myth,

But tread you somewhat fearfully
And treat them with respect
Or else you'll suffer, tearfully,
From what you least expect.

For to the moorland, so they say
Came nineteen maids to feast,
Who dared upon a holy day
Play truant from their priest

And in the grip of devilry
With wildness in their eyes
They came in reckless revelry
With shrill unbridled cries.

Straightway Satan's vipers
Unto the maids came nigh,
Who took the form of pipers
Full seven metres high.

All night long they roistered
And wantonly behaved,
They who once were cloistered
But now could not be saved.

Their souls were torn asunder,
They gave a final groan,
Struck down with deafening thunder,
The maids were turned to stone;

Likewise the devil's servants
Playing their ghostly theme
In abject blind observance
Of Satan's cruel scheme.

The pipers' souls were broken,
They neither sing nor stir;
In stone they but betoken
The giants that they were.

*

Four times the devil did the same
In the wilds of West Penwith,
And four times nineteen maids became
Four times a megalith.

You'll find one at Boscowan-ûn
In gorse and twisted scrub
And bathed in white at each full moon
Its ithyphallic hub.

At Tregeseal on its barren rise
Did the devil again attack
And nineteen perished under the eyes
Of dark Carn Kenidjack

And on Boskednan's lonely moor
Hard by the Mên-an-tol
Each maid became the devil's whore
Ere yielding up her soul.

*

These ancient tales were sent to us
To warn of what they teach,
Whose time is more adventurous
Than lying on the beach

And therefore, girls, be modest, prim,
When abroad in West Penwith,
Lest to these four stone circles grim
You one day add a fifth!

# Reflections On The Death Of My Father

*2007 was overshadowed by the death of my dear father, on 28 July, at the age of 95. He always said he enjoyed reading my verse, although he seemed to think it slightly odd that a member of his family, not known for any tradition of 'creative writing', should show leanings in that direction.*

*I dedicate the next five poems to his memory.*

## (1) Last Stop

'Home', a reassuring word,
Touch down and take on fuel,
But when the article is heard -
'A home'- it can be cruel.

Mostly for our stay on earth
The future's what sustains us,
And since it calibrates our worth
Its absence is what pains us.

The hands are willing, albeit slow,
The brain is still connected,
But the stout old frame I used to know
By God's been de-selected.

You've out-survived contemporaries
Though dearly wish you hadn't,
Extreme old age, let's face it, leaves
Not much but to be saddened.

You want again to climb the hills,
You want to dig the garden,
Relief from geriatric ills,
You beg the gods their pardon.

Two World Wars and not to die
And saw the peacetime crumble,
But was at last to justify
Your slogan – 'mustn't grumble'.

So long the journey, now you've come
To ninety-five and failing,
Those tiny things are troublesome
That used to be plain-sailing.

The future shrinks as grows the past
Our ticket's only *one*-way,
You know this flight will be your last
As you approach the runway.

So here we are, 'a home' is best,
Feel more relief than pity,
You write the cheque, they do the rest
And look – the nurse is pretty!

## (2) Mind And Matter

There came a time,
Lent credence by his rare capacious mind,
When we and all around us -
Getting used to his being always there,
Ensconced in his favourite chair,
Books, papers, batteries for hearing aids,
*Pride and Prejudice*, the TLS,
The European Central Bank Review,
Torch (for power cuts), piles of greeting cards

Stacked on the special table set on castors -
Harboured in a corner of our minds
That here was the exception that proved the rule:
All men are mortal!

At first he was puzzled.
"Tottery" was the word he used, "I'm getting
Tottery", and ascribed it to an illness,
A state which up to then had passed him by.
He took himself off to Mount Alvernia
For an MOT. The surgeons licked their lips
Embarked on an infinitude of tests
And then misled him by their cheerfulness
(Well, that's their job, I suppose)
And told him to expect with confidence
In five years' time
His hundredth birthday missive from the Queen.
We wondered at his misplaced faith in experts
His unexpected gullibility.

I will not chart the steps of his decline
Save that he lost his appetite for food,
He who had relished healthy quantities
Of heavy lunches on our weekly jaunts.
To those who had charge of him
He simply seemed to be recalcitrant,
Failed to co-operate.
But suddenly he seemed to be resolved
And his strength of spirit smouldered into life
As his physical strength began to ebb away.

So he fought to uphold his strategy
With a steely courage that astonished us:
'Mustn't grumble, must accept our fate
And ninety-five's enough!'
Decision made, he simply stuck to it,
Like chairing a meeting at the Treasury
And mouthed in French the sounds that failed to come:

"*Tout doit finir*"

So what remains? A certain sense of shame
That we, his closest confidants,
Could not acknowledge what he clearly saw,
Endorse his strategy and play him straight.
Perhaps we did not know him well enough
To take the risk, and each one has his role,
Like the gallant nurses
Who scolded him and willed him to be good.

Behind the closed eyes and the feeble frame
The disembodied Rolls-Royce mind ground on
Thinking it through;
Could we detect a hint of admonition
That we who were nearest and supposed to know
Failed him at last
Sacrificing our integrity
To uphold the so-called sanctity of life?

## (3) THE THINGS UNSAID

At the ceremony those who spoke
In complementary reminiscences
Came at him in various different ways,
Rounding him out,
Lovable, eccentric, of great substance,
Showing how that massive intellect
Reacted with the ordinary world.

I'd written down my piece then worked on it.
Its peroration was a moving tribute
From a household name, a former Chancellor,
Then ended with five simple, heavy words.

As the time approached
I read it through, mouthing it silently.
All was well: here was my father,
Simplified through art,
Yet with enough to mark him out from others,
Until those five small words,
When my eyes misted over
And the mouthing had to cease.

We then rehearsed our pieces *en famille*
And once more all was well
With mine until those troublesome last words
Emerged with their message strangled, false, distorted.

So the day came
And with it came the need to speak the words.
Just focus on the sound, and not the meaning!
For I had to have them said: memorials
For a brief hour or so evoke fond memories
But must not thereby shut them out for good;
This was no bid to exorcise a ghost
But to define a void that would endure.

Yet as I led up to that final thought
I felt the sluice-gates opening within
And could not, like Macbeth with his 'amen',
Give voice to it.

And so belatedly to keep my vow
To promulgate those words, I say them now:

*"How we shall miss him!"*

## (4) The Butler's Table

The surface is of fine mahogany,
Two brass hinges fixed on each straight edge
Sunk flush into the wood
And joined to thin curved segments
Pierced with hand-shaped holds
Which fold into the perpendicular
To give a tray with sides,
Or turned out flat
They form a perfect oval plane,
Which sits upon a jointed wooden frame
To make a table,
The sort of thing the butler used to use
To bring pre-prandial drinks for dinner guests.

The butler's table
Became the focus of his social gatherings,
On which he placed his recent acquisitions,
Books from Folio,
The latest photo of a great-great-niece,
Or where the tea and sandwiches were laid
(Alas not by the butler),
Or as a means of rising from the chair
By gripping the hand-holds on the table's edge
And with a rocking motion
Launching himself into the vertical.

We eye it warily,
This piece inherited
That's found its way into our living-room,
Such a pregnant symbol of a life
Of one we loved,
Almost alive itself,
Watching, witnessing,
And, who knows, passing judgement
Even from beyond the grave!

# (5) Tiggy

When at last he found himself alone
He knew that what he needed was a cat,
Companion for his ninth and tenth decades
And shortly, from the litter of a friend's,
Acquired one, infinitely cute at first,
Though subsequently on maturity
Exhibiting a certain feistiness,
Arching its back at visitors
And sharpening claws on cherished Persian rugs.

A bond grew up between them,
Not of an over-sentimental kind,
But one of due respect and understanding:
Could not the cat do things *he* could not do
For all his eminence,
Like keeping the apartment free of vermin,
Or voicing its contentedness
By purring after each twice-daily meal?

What use can be the product of a mind,
One that remained so active to the end,
Confined within the head that houses it?
So the cat became his confidant
And if, upon arrival,
You paused a moment just outside the door,
You might have sensed a murmuring within
And heard the cat invited to reflect
Upon some burning issue of the day,
Until the time to end the seminar
And open up another tin of Whiskas.

In summer, in the evening, after supper,
He'd don his hat, take up his walking-stick
And step into the garden.
The cat would slip out as the door was closing

And then in single file they'd both perform
A circumambulation of the grounds,
(Scene that glued the neighbours to their windows!)
The cat maintaining a respectful distance,
Sometimes advancing, sometimes dropping back,
As if tied on to an elastic string.

Whenever the old man stopped and turned
To check the presence of his alter-ego,
The proud cat
Would stop too and assume a grooming posture,
Paw in air, head down, as if to say
"We are not dogs, you know, we cats,
Slavishly to do our master's bidding;
If we wish to take the evening air
We will, and if then by coincidence
Our route turns out identical to his
Do not assume we set a precedent
Or misinterpret motives never meant."

## *LA PETITE GRANGE*

*In memory of a Romanesque-church-crawl in the Dordogne with Nick and Anna*

*La Petite Grange* reposes where
To raise our mood we need no winch,
While in the valley calm *Vézère*
Collects its waters, inch by inch.

In this idyllic spot we see
Nature and man their bargain clinch;
Dreamland or reality?
To know we have ourselves to pinch!

A serious house with humour laced
(Where English folk outnumber Frinch!)
From which, with welcome warm encased,
The pampered guest need never flinch.

Recall when men, with hatred filled,
Each other for their faith would lynch,
But then the prettiest church would build
With squat stone tower and scalloped squinch.

To-day we sit beneath the oak
Where swoop the woodpecker and finch,
In *Côtes de Bergerac* we soak –
To live the good life here's a cinch!

# WHO'S WHO?

*Handel's* Giulio Cesare*: a crib*

Cleopatra thinks Julius Caesar
Of all Roman manhood the pearl;
While Caesar would die just to please her
Although he is sung by a girl

And Sextus, with boldness uncommon,
Of revenge for his father he sings,
But his music is scored for a woman
And he looks like a choirboy from King's.

Behold Cleo's brother, P-tolemy,
A role that is apt to deceive;
His part, though a male (if you follow me)
Is higher than you would believe.

Ah, what a relief is Achilla,
Of his morals one can't be a fan;
He's a sort of Egyptian guerrilla
But he looks as he sounds: like a man.

So don't by the plot get befuddled,
This opera is wholly benign;
The sex is a little bit muddled
But the music is simply divine!

## HAYDN SEEK

In judging folk our interest lies
Not in their professions;
Examine, rather, if you're wise
Their personal obsessions.

While some will cultivate their land
And others dote on pets,
I've joined that esoteric band
Who play in string quartets.

To most the chamber music sect
Remains a world apart;
To us it hones the intellect
And nourishes the heart.

Like other faiths, though secular,
Our ritual's well-rehearsed;
We've one rule in particular:
That Haydn's taken first,

Then, spoilt for choice, we'll have our fling,
So many works are written;
We're game for almost anything
(Save Bartok, Bax and Britten).

We own our rhythm sometimes errs,
Not every chord's in tune,
For faultlessness in amateurs
Is asking for the moon,

And yet we know the goal we seek,
The sound we’re trying to find;
And what we lack in our technique
We make up in the mind.

So hail the Budapest Quartet,
Acclaim the Amadeus,
But measured by the fun *we* get
No others can outplay us!

# WAITING FOR BOZO

*"There is a good chance that the Higgs Boson, the most elusive particle in physics, the missing piece of the 'Standard Model' that describes the building blocks of nature, will be found within the next few years."*

*Press report, April 2008.*

We're tired of the quark and the photon,
We know that we're particle prigs,
But now we cosmologists dote on
The boson suggested by Higgs.

The trouble is – nobody's seen one
Although we have searched high and low;
If we don't track it down it would mean one
Can never explain what we know,

For whenever you come across matter,
Be it solid, or liquid, or gas,
Or whether you're thinner or fatter
This boson's what gives you a mass.

We think it was there for the picking
In that steamy high-density pot
The moment that time started ticking
And all was stupendously hot

But now it is somewhere inside a
Device that will ape the Big Bang,
The awesome Large Hadron Collider,
That hopes of the boson all hang.

Says the Prof, "It's a prospect that thrills me,"
As he sweeps back his wispy white hair;
"I'll never give up if it kills me,
For I know that the bastard is there!"

We'll witness the father-and-mother
Of energies where, at their height,
Protons will clobber each other
At a speed very near that of light

And the Prof, catching sight of his boson,
Will say, "My career is now sealed;
Like a beautiful girl with no clothes on
All has at last been revealed!"

# HARDBACK

Wandering one day through Waterstone's
A warning signal in my lower back
Brought me sharply to a halt
Between *Crime Fiction* and *Biography*
One more step
One tiny movement
And everything was going to fall apart

I stood there stranded
Like an ancient tome with damaged spine
Left on a dusty shelf

After some minutes that dragged on like hours
Mocked by shelves of books all out of reach
The butt of hostile stares
I realised now was not the time for pride
A call for intervention was required
But from which agency –
The human or divine?

The latter option being more discreet
I plumped for it
So summoned up resolve
And mouthed a prayer

Slowly I slid one foot along the floor
Fearing imminent collapse
The structure held
Then gingerly I eased the other foot
In front
Unbending
Looking straight ahead

Step by careful step
Like walking in slow motion on the water
Past the till and through the open door
Into the street

## SLIPPER'D PANTALOON

Writer's block,
State of shock,
Furies beckon, demons mock;
Too much time,
Past one's prime,
Words rebel and refuse to rhyme.

*Have you had a hair-cut,*
*Been to the bank?*
*Checked your e-mails,*
*Topped up the tank?*
*Done your tax form,*
*Watered the beds?*
*Sent a present to the*
*Newly-weds?*

Market's down,
Lawn's gone brown,
Digital image shows a permanent frown;
Life's on hold,
Getting old,
Move our savings into gold?

*Foxed by e-Bay,*
*Can't do blogs,*
*Classical music's*
*Going to the dogs;*
*Dread the outcome*
*Of medical tests,*
*Golden weddings are*
*Nice for the guests.*

Future's black,
Painful back,
Used to please but lost the knack;
Love of late
Sell-by date,
Romantic skies obnubilate.

*Value friendships,*
*Balm to the soul,*
*Alas the Reaper*
*Takes his toll;*
*Humanists not yet*
*Under the sod,*
*Don't be surprised*
*If I turn to God!*

## *WINTERREISE*

*Josef von Spaun remembers*

Well, how were we to know?
"Come", he'd urged us, "come to-night to Schober's,
I've something to surprise you all in song."

For years his fading health had troubled us,
We didn't talk about it much,
The matter being somewhat delicate
And always up to then he'd shrugged it off,
Salvaging his sanity
By writing works that brimmed with happiness.

And so we gathered round his pianoforte
Surprised to sense a graveness in the air,
Somehow aware this evening was to be
No ordinary *Schubertiade*.

He plunged into those fateful, plodding chords
That launch the journey of the Wanderer,
Dragging his voice half-toneless through the score,
Stumbling, halting in the piano part
Like Müller's bleak protagonist himself,
Blinded by frozen tears.
How did he make these strange gloom-ridden songs
Anchored in their searing minor mode
So heart-rending, even when shafts of sunlight
Wrench the music to a major key
To paint rare flashbacks of past ecstasy?

When he stopped
It felt as if the world itself had stopped,
A chasm of despair had opened up
Which threatened to annihilate us all,

Wanderer, audience, even Franz himself,
With only the unhinged hurdy-gurdy man
Our link with life.

One day we'd understand
How great art can ennoble what it treats
And speak of hope while painting hopelessness
And how that evening Schubert spoke the truth.
"I like these songs", he said,
"The time will come when you will like them too."

Alas - embarrassed, puzzled, ignorant,
One by one we tiptoed from the room;
Confronted by his genius we failed.
We did our best, but how were we to grasp
The miracle that we'd been witness to?
We hadn't been prepared:
That agonising journey through the snow,
The phantom images, the mocking crow,
That evening all those many years ago,
At Schober's.

# DINNER AT VANN

*For Mary Caroe*

The air as the sun set was chilling,
For the guests roaming round in the grounds,
But the feast for the eyeballs was thrilling
And the trees rang with avian sounds;
Expanses of pallid camassia
And scented wild garlic galore,
The wooded crevasse here a flowering glacier -
No-one could envy it more.

So back from the garden, elated,
The inglenook hearth we embraced
And the warmth of the welcome negated
The numbness our bodies had faced;
Pre-prandial drinks started flowing
Which enhanced the effects of the fire,
Our faces were glowing from gen'rous Bordeaux-ing
(Or was it from mutual desire?)

From the walls of the oak-panelled parlour
The talk ricochet-ed like a gun:
Was Mendelssohn greater than Mahler?
Was Dryden more gifted than Donne?
We spoke of some radical thinkers,
Our travels in Uzbekistan,
The fate of the Incas, the rare oxyrhinchus,
The pleasures of dinner at Vann.

# THOSE LEFT BEHIND

*For Gentian in memory of Michael Hodges (1936-2009)*

"It must be such a shock for you", she said,
"You'd seen him in his normal element
Only a week before." Indeed we had,
Quaffing his usual village burgundy,
Considerate, courteous, laying down the law,
Making us laugh.

A shock indeed
And noble thoughts of love and sympathy
Struggled with less noble ones
Like hurt, resentment, even bitterness,
For he was always in our calendar;
Each date we made was like
A ticket to a life-affirming play,
An entertainment somehow ours of right.

And now a thread from life's rich tapestry
Has suddenly frayed and snapped
Unravelling the fabric of our lives;
Mortality, that priest of finitude,
Who gives our time its purpose and its bounds,
Creeps upon us with its black-lined purse
To seize its deadly rent.

She who is left behind, (what strength she has!)
Concerned at how *we*'d take the dreadful news,
Sorry to have deprived us of a friend,
Faced with a huge void swallowing her life,
Finds pity for the lesser one in ours.

## THE VANISHING FLOAT

From charges of hilarity
Our milkman is exempt;
He shuns familiarity
For fear it breeds contempt.

From normal intercourse he flees
Whom idle gossip irks;
We speak a kind of milkman-ese
And here is how it works:

The bottle-neck's the medium
Through which our greetings flow,
Three times a week the bottles come:
His way to say 'hello'.

A silver top says "full of cream",
A red says "semi-skimmed";
Though cool recipients we seem,
Our sympathy's undimmed.

We leave the empty bottles bright
Outside, we know it ranks
In milkmen's minds as just the right
Routine for saying 'thanks',

But when no empty's waiting there
Outside upon the ground
He feels a sort of dull despair
That blights his morning round

And then I pen a friendly note
Rolled up inside a bottle,
Which sends him happy on his float
Revived, fulfilled, full-throttle.

*

You milkmen in your country lanes
To-day's consumer spurns;
Yours was the time of steam-powered trains
When milk was poured from churns.

You ply your trade – for how long more?
Your fate's to 'progress' linked;
Ubiquitous, the superstore
Is making you extinct.

Now ancient trades are laughed to scorn
As each its end awaits
And when you've vanished, who will mourn
The clatter of your crates?

## UNNATURAL SELECTION

The ostrich has evolved all wrong,
A cul-de-sac it's found;
It flaps its wings so hard and long
But never leaves the ground.

When on a courtship mission they
Contort their snaky necks,
But God knows what position they
Adopt for having sex.

Yet of the creatures from the ark
The ostrich has my vote;
It is, though uglier than the lark,
More useful than the stoat.

You utilise its carapace
Of leather as a source;
Its feathers can adorn your face,
Some ride it like a horse

And those whose taste for steak is keen
The ostrich will sustain;
While if you like nouvelle cuisine
Try pickled ostrich brain.

In Mrs Beeton's recipes
Four dozen eggs were due;
She should have used the ostrich's
And needed only two!

As pet this bird could scarcely feel
Less cuddlesome or ruder,
But roaming round your garden he'll
Discourage the intruder.

A pretty sight they do not make,
But shouldn't take the blame;
They're evolution's big mistake –
I love them all the same.

# The Coffin

*For Romi in memory of Michael Tunstall-Behrens (1923-2009)*

We knew it would dig deep this funeral
Too deep to encompass on the day itself
Here was a man of rarest quality
Not because he conquered enemies
Or opened out the frontiers of science
Nor because he changed the world
(Indeed he sought to keep the world unchanged
That which was worth conserving)
But for his awesome spirit

From earliest years he'd looked about him
Gaining the measure of his fellow men
Then gifted with his Cornish heritance
Defended it with passionate seriousness
While relishing the ironies of life
The contradictions, the absurdities
Poking fun at life's pomposities
So that his countenance
As school-boy or as weather-beaten sage
Lit up by a smile
Though never a soft touch or with false regard
Could captivate before a word exchanged

He had an instinct for the apt and true
As when embarked on fashioning a gate
He'd use old oak re-cycled from a wreck
Cross-pieces worked to the family monogram
Planed and jointed with old-fashioned mortises
Made to withstand the great Atlantic gales

This craftsmanship was passed down to his heir
And worked into the sturdy pinewood coffin
Shaped like some ocean-going barque
With stout rope handles hanging from the sides
And there it rested on a simple trailer
Drawn by tractor steered by a grieving son
Slowly across the fields and up the hill
With booted mourners following behind
Whence strong men bore it to the hallowed ground
At the cliff's edge

Fashioned on a single valveless horn
The searing Britten Tenor Serenade
Sang his spirit to its resting-place
To the moan of surf pounding the rocks below
And as the coffin sank into the earth
Those assembled on the promontory
Watched – silhouetted by the sinking sun
Like golden-haloed angels in a cloud –
A dynasty in solemn pantomime
Move one more frame along the reel of time.

# PART 4 - POEMS 2010-2014

## Noble Rot

Fifty-odd miles to the south of Bordeaux
Is the source of a secret I happen to know;
From the swamps that the oaks of the *Landes* feed upon
There bubbles a spring that becomes the *Ciron.*

This cold little stream as it washes *Sauternes*
For the feel of the warmer *Garonne* starts to yearn
And as the two climates together converge
Precipitate mists in the valleys emerge.

These damp autumn days, when at last they arrive,
Encourage the fungus *Botrytis* to thrive
That shrivels and rots the ripe fruit on the vine,
Creating the heaven unique to this wine.

The cull in the vineyards extends many weeks:
No bunch can be picked till its rottenness peaks,
A labour-intensity sadly that shows
In the price of a bottle – you pay through the nose!

It's born to a fanfare of cymbals and brass
Sunshine and laughter and sin in a glass,
Apricots, pineapple, crystallised peel,
Flavours of decadence tempered with steel.

*Châteaux Haut-Peyraguey, Climens, d'Yquem,*
Oenology's treasure, its liquefied gem;
Amber when young, then a glorious gold
And glowing in butterscotch bronze when it's old.

So slice some *foie gras* from the *Périgord Noir*,
Uncork the *Sauternes* and rise up and awa';
Trumpet the tributes from Tours to Toulon:
Here's to the magic of little *Ciron*!

# THE YORKSHIRE PENSIONERS

*'This tablet was erected by the officers and nurses of the 116th General Hospital of the United States army, who, serving their country during World War II, spent many happy days in Harrogate and enjoyed the hospitality of all Yorkshire. 28th July, 1944'*

*Memorial Stone in Valley Gardens, Harrogate*

Up and down in Yorkshire there are many who survive
Who share in certain attributes: their age is sixty-five
And furthermore, in spite of their diversity, they seem
Proud owners of a middle name that has a common theme:

'Albuquerque', 'Atlanta', 'Arizona', 'Arkansas',
Christened at the ending of the Second World War;
'Denver', 'Dallas', 'Davenport'; 'Dayton', 'Delaware',
The home towns of the fathers of these pensioners were there!

For many of the officers their fate, alas, was dark,
But not before in Harrogate and Hull they'd left their mark;
For all these Yankee names convey, in truth it is no joke,
The bounteous hospitality of Yorkshire's womenfolk.

# CORNISH TRIP

Winter week-end dash to Truro
Feel the promise of the sea;
Cornish landscape chiaroscuro
Prospects good as they could be.

Coated, booted, convoy rally
Wading through the coast-path mud;
Stumbled climbing out of valley
Lay spread-eagled, caked in crud.

Plodded onward, suspect ankle
Body shaken, spirits dull;
God's unfairness cause to rankle
Mocked by cormorant and gull.

Limped a mile of painful paces
Friendly transport rescues me;
Find restorative oasis
Perranuthnoe's hostelry.

Tried to shrug it off, no telling
Wasn't keen to let them down;
Eyed with awe the growing swelling
Plan tomorrow's trip to town.

*

Proudly stands the Royal Cornwall
Eager waits its A&E;
Poised to treat, if not to warn all
Feckless wanderers like me.

Tell Admissions my disaster
Wheeled around from stage to stage;
Admin, screening, X-ray, plaster
Each procedure takes an age.

Finally the diagnosis
"Fractured fibula" they say;
Plus, what makes me more morose is
"Ankle wrenched, the joint a-splay."

Need an early operation
Hurry eastward through the night;
Morning, I'm again a patient
Guildford must resolve my plight.

Nine-hour wait in grim surroundings
Day that every patient dreads;
Plausible are their expoundings
Too much trauma, too few beds.

Comes at last the surgeon, Gossage,
Outlines plan to cut and set;
(Says his surname rhymes with sausage
Just in case I might forget).

Wheel-chair ride to campus fringes
Dark outside through rain and sleet;
Here's the ward, forget my whinges
Home-from-home and this one's sweet.

Pale blue curtains drawn, I'm hidden
Notice warns 'No Food to Take';
Even water is forbidden
Evil thoughts of fillet steak.

Now consultant's pre-op visit
Acolytes hail every quip;
"Well", he booms, "It's painful, is it?
Let us call it 'Cornish Trip!'"

Taken finally to theatre
Drug-man problems finding vein;
Fight the potion, drawing near to
Deeds that make me well again.

Convalescent, chained to crutches
Drained of normalcy and pep;
Fate spares neither dog nor duchess
Blame the gods – and mind your step!

# Sky Lanterns

*For Georgie and Pete*

My bids to find employment have for many years been spurned,
So picture my excitement now at last my luck has turned;
I've landed my first offer since they put me out to grass:
'Assistant Vice Unpacker of Sky Lanterns (Second Class)'.

My bosses wouldn't pay me as I wasn't very skilled,
But they'd give me board and lodging – I was genuinely thrilled;
They promised that the benefits inherent in my role
Were much more satisfactory than life upon the dole.

I turned up at my workplace feeling diligent and keen,
They handed me the biggest box of lanterns ever seen;
They told me not to worry, that I'd soon be having fun,
So with a heavy heart I started lantern number one.

At first I couldn't crack it, every lantern needed fire
From impregnated wadding to be fixed in place by wire;
It seemed my job description had been hopelessly misjudged
And not a single training course – a lapse that I begrudged.

A certain skill was needed, but it seemed I simply lacked it,
Yet gradually, I'm proud to say, by sweat and toil I cracked it;
So after just an hour or two, and though I was untrained,
A lantern had been done and only fifty-nine remained!

I worked for many hours and saw my output rate improve,
Till after thirty lanterns I was really in the groove,
By forty-five, they said, I was exhibiting some flair
And I satisfied the deadline with a little time to spare.

*

The lanterns they were beautiful, so fast they rose, so high,
I shed a little tear as they lighted up the sky;
To crown it all, my bosses have promoted me a stage:
'Chief Packer of Spent Lanterns', with a statutory wage.

## BEVAGNA OR BUST

To Cornwall and to Cumbria
Farewell, we're off to Umbria,
Its myriad attractions we've absorbed by word of mouth;
Abandoning the Tuscans
For the land of the Etruscans,
We have hired an Opel Astra and are heading for the South.

To fix our mental vista, we
Have swotted up our histor-y:
Our knowledge of medieval art is virtually complete;
And as to the Renaissance
We are verging on complacence –
But alas we hadn't counted on the fierce Italian heat.

From a *quattrocento* Mecca
To the next *pinacoteca*
We are trudging up steep alleyways and panting for the shade;
We lurch round Orvieto
And the churches of Spoleto
But confuse them with each other as our strength begins to fade.

Such wealth of *Pinturicchios*!
You have to take your pick, he owes
His fame to *Perugino* with whose art he has a link;
Their legacy was lasting
Though their styles are quite contrasting
But they're hard to disentangle if you're dying for a drink.

Our visit to *Assisi,*
So reputed, made us queasy
As the famous *Giotto* frescoes clearly visible were not;
For the pilgrim to St Francis

Seething tourists don't enhance his
Delectation if they're crowding out the paintings, and it's hot.

We trudged around *Bevagna*
Where it couldn't have been sunnier,
Making sure there were no cultural attractions we might miss;
But enough of *Cimabue* -
While the heat is *trentadue*
We are staying by the swimming pool where ignorance is bliss!

## ON FIRST LOOKING INTO BALDOCK'S 'WASPS OF SURREY'

*For David Baldock, with admiration*

*(After Keats's Chapman's Homer, with the same rhyming scheme)*

Much have I travelled on wild, rugged heath
Where Frensham, Churt and Puttenham's sandy slopes
Lend entomologists their cherished hopes
Of unrecorded insects. Up on Leith
Or on the dry south-facing banks beneath
I laboured to appease my microscopes,
Yet knew I not the Hymenopteral ropes
Until on Baldock's *Wasps* I cut my teeth.
Then felt I like some bearded anorak
When a new genus swims before his lens,
Or like Linnaeus on a new-found tack
His murky taxonomic scheme to cleanse,
Conquering the evidential lack
Of proven links to Homo Sapiens.

# FREE FLOW

*Lines on the opening of the Hindhead tunnel*

Were we non-corporeal like neutrinos,
We'd mimic the trajectory the bee knows
And fly straight through the hill, with no entreaty
For massive public funds, no Balfour Beatty.

Alas we harbour mass, so rain or shine
The Hindhead bottleneck flowed, not like wine
But as detritus through a half-blocked drain,
Back-snaking waves that stop, go, stop again.

Our senses taut, we sought release from tension
To find inside our hill a third dimension
And weigh the liberated space exposed
With that which went before, now juxtaposed.

Pale faces in the Chunnel, long and lost,
Find no feeling worthy of its cost,
But here the diggers triumphed to construct
A route as thrilling as a viaduct.

We welcomed first the humorous 'toothpaste tubes'
Jutting from the cliff like hollow boobs
And once inside could trace the Punchbowl's curve
(Full speed ahead and keep a steady nerve!)

And then, as if by master playwright cued,
(No time to stick in troglodytic mood)
Fast from the southern portal we emerged,
The A3's constipation fully purged.

So in this violation of a hill
We find the benefit outweighs the ill
And gain some glimpses at this opening beano
Of life viewed by the substanceless neutrino.

## THE USE OF BISCUITS

***Oldie Competition No. 134***
*"One of the stranger aspects of Gordon Brown's premiership was his uncertainty about which biscuits he liked. Perhaps he had no use for them. So a poem, please, called 'The Use of Biscuits'. Maximum 16 lines"*

In my bid to save the world I called on Berlusconi,
His arguments against me were, I have to say, baloney;
But Silvio has a weakness for his entourage of totty:
I knew that he'd surrender when they plied him with *biscotti*.

Next in line was *Sar*kozy – his flattery was pleasing,
I urged on him the benefits of quantitative easing;
At first he wouldn't toe the line, he thought the plan too risky,
But Carla overruled him as she handed out *les biscuits*.

Lastly off to Germany to visit Mrs Merkel
With whom it wasn't hard to square the economic circle,
For though she has no hang-ups with regard to either sex,
She's something of a pushover when gorging on *die Keks*.

To Downing Street they come from all the corners of the earth,
I give them with their barley water oatcakes made in Perth;
It's not that they don't wish to call my policies in question,
They simply cannot fight both me and Scottish indigestion!

## Taj Mahal

A parakeet sat in a deodar tree
Preening itself, ‘Look at me! Look at me!
Turn from an artefact fashioned by men,
Mark me a God-given ten-out-of-ten!’

Mumtaz, the chosen of Emperor Jahan
Whose love was the greatest since loving began,
Perished in childbirth; the order was tough:
‘The world’s finest shrine will be scarcely enough’.

‘Frozen in marble, a teardrop of love
On the cheek of eternity’, heavens above!
A thing that is born while the great Homer nods
Can rival the creatures designed by the gods.

Grey, pink and yellow, then dazzling white,
The dome cedes to Allah its soft play of light;
Within the vast chamber mysterious looms
A heavenly lid for the simplest of tombs.

When you gaze at the Taj with its jewel-studded forms
Soaring beyond architectural norms,
You cannot but pity the wretched conceit
Of that conquered-in-beauty, the poor parakeet!

# THURSDAY COFFEE

*The smiling Virgin, Chateau Comtal, Carcassone*

Wrapped in stone through seven centuries,
Now brought down from some high altarpiece
To mingle with the people,
She wears her infant like a badge of honour,
Not flaunting her divinity,
Nor with affectation of demureness,
But smiling, bearing her stupendous role
With equanimity.

Marking how her humour, her humanity
Lightens the tread of every passer-by,
I picture her at Thursday morning coffee
Proudly swapping tales of motherhood:
“So there I was,
And when my visitors, the Kings, had gone
I bathed his feet in oil of frankincense
Poured from a golden chalice...!”

# The Bubble

*Jessica Ennis-Hill, Heptathlete, Olympic gold medal, London, 2012*

What we looked for in the Games was glamour,
On pommel-horse, in hurdles, hockey, hammer,
But who are the special ones we took most to our hearts,
What puts them in a class apart?
Not just the golds, the silvers, and the bronzes,
Not just their scores, their nationalities, beyond this
Some quality which holds them down to earth and wins
Our true devotion for these super-specimens.

Take Jess, heptathlete, with the modest air,
The load we'd placed on her almost too much to bear,
Emblazoned everywhere, Team GB's effigy,
As if she owed it to her worshippers to heed their plea
That one frail-looking girl assume the strength of granite,
That she should be the greatest on the planet!

Confronted with this stress she'd not abhor it,
Neither strike an attitude, nor just ignore it,
But weave a sort of bubble round herself
Through which could only (for her mental health)
Flow images of what would shape her marks:
The mocking hurdles, the concentric arcs
By means of which is done each ruthless calculation,
While the huge crowd, with a roar of expectation,
Is silenced by the bubble.

She crouches, shutting out the rabble.

Off goes the gun and at the gun goes Jess,
Slaying the hurdles with a 100-metre best
Of twelve-point-five-four seconds, then she high-jumped
A decent one-point-eight-six at her third attempt

And then the shot, which this Olympic waif
Put fourteen metres, twenty-eight – surely she's safe?
Then adds a lightning 200 metres sprint – no trouble.

At each success she steps out briefly from the bubble
To acknowledge the acclaim
And then as quickly steps back in again.

Her nose in front with three events to go,
Now all is hers – and all is hers to blow!
Come on! Come on now! Grab the moment, Ennis!
(Think of Andy Murray in the tennis!)

Long jump respectable, so far so fine
Then follows the javelin, a record forty-seven, four-nine
And now she's virtually destroyed the field,
For the eight-hundred she only needs to trot to make them yield,
But that is not the way she wants to be,
Her face is scary in its fixity.

At last she's off, leading from the start,
Is overtaken, then, flaunting the true heptathlete's art,
Claws back the lead in a prolonged and glorious burst
To finish first.

The bubble pops, the tears and smiles and hugs,
A wave of joy at seventy thousand heartstrings tugs
And at the altar of the assembled media
She offers the crowd her thanks for helping her.

What comes across – so simple, honest, sure,
So – dare I say it? – little-girl-next-door;
Therein resides the glamour of this athlete bent
Upon her one and glorious intent.

Now round her neck the proof, the golden treasure,
“I’m glad I gave so many so much pleasure,
But do not offer more than is my due:
Others have their good days at the office too!”

## DELPHINIUMS

Survey the border with a single glance
Between the pampered lawn and ancient wall
Under June's high-angled sun:
The blowsy English rose, the peony,
The scarlet poppies smudged with black
Like giant upturned ladybirds,
The outrageous crambe with its fireball flowers,
The pincushions of wild geranium.

Even this bed that shouts the summer out
Would fail but for its backing range
Of proud delphinium peaks
That give the stamp of authenticity
To all true plots that claim herbaceousness!

Regard the blues:
Electric, Midnight, Royal, Violet,
But one above the others, quintessential,
An Innocent *light-sky* blue
(And each small floret with an eye of white)
Whose function here transcends florality
Embodying a thousand images -
Of party frocks, straw boaters and the thwack
Of ball on racket past the hornbeam walk –
As if a swatch of sky
Sewn with points of tiny sunlit clouds
Had cloned itself to form an intricate
Kaleidoscopic tapestry.

# Bowcott Hill

Its banks are ranged like gothic stalls
Beneath a bare-root vaulted nave
Where shards of old retaining walls
Betray the tales the years engrave

For in this steep and sunken lane
The essence of each season lies
And through its emblems we ordain
A micro-world in rural guise

As following a springtime shower
The lane becomes a tributary
That speeds the infant River Ar
Along its journey to the sea

Or shafts of sunlight strained through leaves
That prick the lane with coins of light
Where deepest summer shadow weaves
A blanket for a noonday night

And as the branches shed their loads
The lane is lit with autumn's rays
Like street-lights lining urban roads
Adjust for ever-shortening days

And finally midwinter's snow
That holds us captive in the drive
But on the ice where children go
Their laughter keeps the lane alive.

# The Beach Tree

Far up the haunches of the great Glen Esk
The waters gather out of Easterballoch,
Spilling foam over leaping salmon
Toiling towards their distant spawning-grounds,
Then hurtling down through Edzell, Marykirk,
Dragging huge clumps of driftwood to the bay
Where North Sea currents sweep them up the coast
To leave their calling cards at high water
Along the infinite St Cyrus sands.

Most of them are sucked back out to sea
And where they go, if not to Neptune's saw-mills,
Who can say? Save for a single pile
Of bare, outlandish shapes
That wind and tide have rooted in the sand,
Immovable, and through its lifelessness –
Upon this calm late autumn day
With clear skies painting a pastel mount
Of silvered pinks and blues, the distant sea
Now calm, unthreatening –
The stark, still tree
Becomes a symbol of the things whose absence
Grips the mind:

The gales that sweep down from the river's source,
Shaving the margins of the forest slopes
And the angry, raging substance of the sea
Shuddering in its depths,
Where strange clawed creatures shift uneasily,
Sensing even in their fastnesses
Those battles in the elemental war
That lay eternal siege upon the shore.

# COSTA RICA CONVERSION

We went to Costa Rica to enjoy a wildlife fix,
We lived a life of blamelessness with Nature for our kicks;
My friends they saw the Frigate Bird, so graceful on the wing,
But with my dud binoculars I didn't see a thing.

They saw the Boat-billed Heron and the Hummingbirds white
collars,
But even if you offered me a hundred thousand dollars
I couldn't spot a Toucan or identify a Vulture,
Coming as I do from a benighted urban culture.

We visited the institute of tropical research,
They saw the Narranjilla tree, the Heron on its perch,
The cheeky Long-tailed Blackbird and the purple Gallinule,
But I just gave up looking and I felt a bloody fool.

To penetrate the forest where the Great Potoo resides
Make sure you go with Ronald - he's the greatest of the guides,
For thrills you'll never tire of and for wonders you will see
Unless you're so unlucky as to happen to be me.

We went to Tortuguero by a jungle waterway,
They photographed the Black-necked Stilt and Sandpipers at play;
They saw a River Otter and a full-grown Cayman pose
While I just gently closed my eyes and had a little doze.

But then in Monteverde in the forest canopy
I spied the famous Quetzal on an avocado tree:
A life-changing experience - like first when you are kissed
And now I'm training up to be an ornithologist.

# Legal Eagle

*'For the purposes of this part of this Schedule a person over pensionable age, not being an insured person, shall be treated as an employed person if he would be an insured person were he under pensionable age and would be an employed person were he an insured person.'*

*Extract from the Statutes*

Our departmental lawyers owned a soft spot in our hearts,
More skill and lower wages than their City counterparts;
The public service ethic still with them walked proud and tall
And my hero, Henry Woodhouse, was the doyen of them all.

*

The Transport Acts were firmly in his massive head installed,
So fast was his advice that 'Same-Day-Cleaning' he was called;
When challenged on some fiendish text he'd say, 'That's for the
birds,
I'd merely change the meaning if I simplified the words'.

Towards each Secretary of State his loyalties were bent,
He saw them as the symbols of the Queen in Parliament;
But those who came to fill the post, though not exactly dud,
Were all a disappointment in their actual flesh and blood.

He didn't suffer fools though he was kind to new recruits,
A notice on his desk would turn the boldest into mutes:
"To those who wisdom seek here, from the North or from the South,
Please ensure your brain's engaged when operating mouth."

*

Our departmental lawyers were an admirable breed,
Immune to sycophancy, insusceptible to greed;
In intellect they largely ranged across the normal span
But my hero, Henry Woodhouse, was the Einstein of the clan.

## WRITER'S BLOCK

O fair poetic Muses, visit me,
You limbs of Zeus and of Mnemosynë,
Guardians of your literary flock –
Come, free this wordsmith from his writer's block!

*Calliope,* who on your tablet gives
An endless stream of rhyming narratives,
Despite the lesser forms upon my shelf
I'd with your help try epic verse myself.

A rose-red crown *Erato* does adorn,
Who pens erotic verse not far from porn;
O that you might seduce me with your lyre
And fill my arid wells with lovers' fire!

Or you, wan elegiac maid, *Euterpe*,
Whose output is indeed more sad than chirpy,
Yet, heroine to those in widows' weeds,
Your tutelage could satisfy my needs.

Last *Polyhymnia* with your sacred verse
Compose some rhymes to strew upon a hearse,
Intone a prayer, invoke a deity –
O fair poetic Muses, visit me!

# War Stopped Play

August the third of that doom-laden summer.
On the big stage armies mobilised
To cut each other down,
While in the little village of The Lee
Cricketers were gathered on the Green -
Eleven from the stately manor house,
Weekend guests of Ivor Liberty,
Heir to the founder of the London store,
Of Buckinghamshire's gilded youth the hub –
Against eleven from the village club.

The match got under way, so did the rain,
Confining play to momentary bursts
Between the squalls, until the weather won.
As Ivor Liberty surveyed the ground
With Arthur Phillips, captain of the village,
They made a pledge
And solemnly resolved to carry on
As soon as the hostilities were done;
Not long to wait until, so they all said,
The War to End all Wars was put to bed.

*

Of seven hundred Lee inhabitants
Thirty men were slaughtered in the trenches,
Many in nineteen-sixteen at Fromelles;
Ivor lost a leg, Arthur was killed,
Two other members of the village team
Never returned
And when at last the dreadful war was over
There seemed more pressing things to fret about
Than resurrect another kind of fight
And one so infinitely slight.

*

But now the current club's vice-President,
Descendent of those earlier Libertys,
Encouraged by the trend
To celebrate our great centenaries,
Has visited the Fromelles cemetery
And scooped a little soil from every grave
Where those young villagers were laid to rest,
These, as symbols of the men who died,
To feature in a contest re-commenced
Between their present-day equivalents.

The game will freeze upon the stroke of four,
A minute's silence as opposing sides
Honour the caskets laid upon the pitch,
Each one the focus of their silent thoughts
Of those brave souls whose selfless actions tamed
Our urge to fight, that it might one day yield
To gentle rituals on a cricket field.

# SICILIAN VESPAS

*Memories of a tour guided by Antonio Marretta,*
*3-17 May 2014*

**Etna**, vast peak of *Sicilia,*
As you climb goes from hot to much chillier;
The isle from so high
Looks as flat as a pie
But in fact it's considerably hillier.

A venue there never has been a
More crowded than old **Taormina**;
You find you must queue
Just to get a good view
And you'd better book early for dīnner.

It was tiring in hot **Agrigento**
Though progress was measured and *lento;*
At the start of the day
I felt *ventitré*,
But when it was done – more like *cento.*

Whenever I'm in **Siracusa**
I feel like a bit of a loser;
Those cultural peaks
Of fourth century Greeks
Are harder to grasp than Medusa.

We arrived at the site of **Segesta**
When I normally take my siesta,
But the wealth of wild flowers
Kept me gazing for hours
At this stunning botanic fiesta.

Our feelings of awe only grew
As we turned off to see **Cefalu**;
Nothing prosaic,
Its stunning mosaic
Was surely our number-one view.

But, Antonio, I must confess a
Feeling of guilt, O Professor,
Confusing Phoenicians
With Romans and Grecians,
But here's to your island – God bless her!

# Reunion Blues

*A poem on the subject 'A reunion from hell', maximum 16 lines, Spectator Competition No. 2837*

In fifty years no fundamental change
Save for the lineaments of age that range,
Etched by time's stylus on the wheel of fate,
From one grey to another's balding pate.

I strive to calibrate their present views
Against their past, while they intone their news
("My youngest grandson's now the Cambridge cox!")
And line their pills up from a plastic box.

For most, it seems, their adolescent ways,
Not always worthy of the highest praise,
Have little more than held a course that is
Along original trajectories

And so the bores became avuncular,
The gourmands and the soaks carbuncular
And as they set about their gala dinns
I watch the juices dribble down their chins.

# PART 5 - POEMS 2015-2020

# BIG CAT

*A trip to Sri Lanka with 'Explore' – 25 Jan to 7 Feb 2016*

To launch our guided survey of Sri Lanka's Great Outdoors
We climbed aboard a cavalcade of rugged four-by-fours
To penetrate the secrets of Wilpattu National Park,
As eager as a physicist who's hunting down a quark.

We saw a Serpent Eagle that was lunching on a snake,
The proud Black-Headed Ibis and the Storks around the lake,
The plump White-Throated Kingfisher and lofty Black-Winged Stilt,
The iridescent Bee-Eater with plumage like a quilt.

A solitary elephant was showering in the reeds,
The wild boars were foraging according to their needs,
The crocodiles lay waiting for their prey to come to hand
While slithery land-monitors just monitored the land.

The tropic sunlight glinted through a wall of white-barked trees
That lent the living corridor a kind of fairy frieze,
But something still was missing from our great safari quest:
The right dramatic climax that would out-perform the rest.

Suddenly commotion halts the progress of our mission,
A traffic-jam of open jeeps all jostling for position;
Could we have reached, we asked ourselves, the forest's *fête champêtre*,
The final confirmation of our journey's *raison d'être*?

*There* now, can you see it, charismatic, salt-and-peppered,
Reclining in a bushy tree, one large and lordly leopard!
And like some godly presence that we humans are beneath
It stared at us disdainfully and bared its massive teeth.

We rattled back along the track, all somewhat in a daze,
Coveting an image that upon the mind still plays;
For since the time my interest in ecology was born
Nothing beats the day we saw that lovely leopard yawn.

# Last Sailing

Two wooden dinghies too ravaged to mend
Lie in the woodland awaiting their end,
Each a loved symbol of days that are past
With boat in the water and sails at the mast.

One was a Firefly, an aristocrat,
The boat-builder's art comes no higher than that;
We called it Columbia, named on a whim
And its lines were enhanced with mahogany trim.

The other, a Mirror, was cheerful and cheap,
It wasn't the quickest of boats on the deep,
So we christened it Tachyon which, if I'm right,
Is a particle travelling faster than light.

*

To witness what holiday rapture can be
Take a dinghy, some boys and a wide-open sea,
For every midsummer the trip they liked most
Was trailing the boats to the West Country coast.

But like other passions, this one had its day,
Those maritime love affairs dwindled away;
We dumped the poor boats in their new parking-lot
And slowly but surely they started to rot.

*

We knew for our dinghies the outlook was bleak,
Their spirit though willing, their flesh was too weak;
So what had been 'living' was clearly now 'late'
And both of the boats we would have to cremate.

Hark! Could we hear the faint keening of gulls
As our merciless chain-saw ripped into the hulls?
With guilty bloodthirstiness, higher and higher
We piled up the parts and set light to the pyre.

*

The embers died down like the Cheshire Cat's grin,
An ash-heap with unconsumed metal bits in;
Now sail up in heaven: our prayers will not cease,
Columbia, Tachyon, rest you in peace!

# THE MOLE MAN

The 'little gentleman in black velvet',
Self-effacing star of Grahame's odyssey,
Too handsome to be vermin,
Too gentle to evoke much wrath,
Yet regicide,[2] pest, saboteur,
Desecrator of well-tended lawns,
Has paid a visit, bringing his friends along.

So now here comes the mole man,
Who loves the countryside
But understands the order of the world:
Who eats who, who *should* eat who but doesn't,
Brandishing traps.

He strives to understand my patch of land
As a taupian universe:
Where the runs are, where the water is,
Where the worms, moles' diet, will assemble,
Where are the abandoned settlements
And disused larders,
Where fresh piles of soil
Mark out the front line of the moles' advance
And where the little tunnellers will strike out next.

So here begins a war
Involving one large, multi-purpose brain
Against one tiny but superbly focussed one.

Because the predatory chain is not in balance
And because the mole man treats his adversary
As one to be respected, if outwitted,

---

[2] William III died in 1702 from a fall from his horse which stumbled on a molehill. For many years afterwards his Jacobite enemies would raise their glasses to "the little gentleman in the black velvet waistcoat."

He's little troubled by a Jainian conscience
Nor does he seek in rural North-East Hants
Nirvana through abjuring violence.

And when a trap goes off,
Snuffing out a life so clinically,
He bears no malice, harbours no triumphalism
As, on the following day,
He strides across the lawn, now sanitised,
Cradling three furry, lifeless forms
In one gloved hand,
And in the other empty traps to yield
The next mole corpses down in Petersfield.

# DE-EXTINCTION

*"Mammoths to be created in two years," say scientists.*
*Press Report, Feb. 2017*

The woolly mammoth fought so hard four thousand years ago
Its tenuous survival to defend,
Till, swallowed by the tundra as it sank beneath the snow,
It became a zoological dead-end.

But scientists from Harvard know the mammoth's DNA
Closely to the elephant's is linked;
They'll use genetic wizardry to act in such a way
That mammoths will be rendered 'de-extinct'.

'We started with this creature', their professor has observed,
'Since mammoths from the grave have lots to tell;
The permafrost refrigerator's happily preserved
Their carcasses astonishingly well.'

First he'll make a *mammophant*, though many problems loom
Before he has the embryo he'd wish;
He really needs an elephant and access to its womb,
But probably he'll grow it in a dish.

A scientific triumph the professor then will taste
When mammoths have been rescued from their plight;
Their bellows will ring out anew across the frozen waste
And not a hunter-gatherer in sight!

So now when the extinction of a species is a threat
The lab will offer skills that Nature lacks:
The Warty Pig, the Stub-Foot Toad, the Red-Necked Avocet,
Defying evolution's cul-de-sacs.

# THY NEIGHBOUR'S ASS

*"Thou shalt not covet thy neighbour's house, thou shalt not covet thy neighbour's wife, or his manservant, or his maidservant, or his ox, or his ass, or anything that is thy neighbour's."*

My friend leads a life of resplendence
(Do I envy his fortune? Not half!)
With wife number three in attendance
And an army of living-in staff.

Another friend's planted a pine-copse
And loves to be riding to hounds;
His newly electrified line stops
The riff-raff invading his grounds.

One has a stone-wall enclosure
Where he grows all his fruit and his veg,
Whose walls minimise the exposure
It would otherwise get with a hedge.

One has a view of the City
From a mansion on high Hampstead Heath;
It's out of my class, more's the pity -
Even the basement beneath.

One has a huge oleander
In a garden he rates as his 'land';
Another a cliff-top veranda
With a seagull's-eye view of the sand.

*

We all play our cards as they reach us,
The good and the bad and the odd,
Believing the sages who teach us
We all are the same before God.

# WHO LIKES BUTTER?

*For Ida, aged 2 years and 2 months*

Yes, they are precious, these *ranunculi*,
Spread like butter on Wittenham Clumps,
But so are you, and more:
In you they focus down
To one small radiant ball of hope,
Framed in sunshine.

Yet, though so newly minted,
Barely two summers' worth of consciousness,
Look deep into that face
And see indeed
Instinctive artless rapture
Among the overwhelming buttercups:
But on another plane
A knowing that you had a part to play,
Like an actress
Conveying the formal concept of pure innocence
That, being so conveyed,
Is pure no more!

# Time's Arrow

My first memory was of long faces
Leaning over me
Sighing backwards
As I surfaced after the long sleep

Leaden I felt, but with hope
For there seemed a strengthening
As the body smoothed itself
And waved the honest nursing staff away

The best thing, the reunion with my kin
Then giving back the walking-stick
Having no further need of it
And strangely everything seemed pre-ordained

When I'm young enough, I said
I want to triumph in heroic feats
Beginning at the winning tape alone
Arriving all together at the start,

Relish that first kiss and its memory
Ever more vivid as I came to it
Welcoming innocence yet knowing the reverse
And the birth of life-long friendships lightly made

So those around me
And all of planet Earth grew younger
Until my children one by one
Mysteriously disappeared

My final memory was of broad faces
Leaning over the cradle
Laughing backwards
As I entered on a second long deep sleep

# The Buzzard

*Lines for Anna in memory of Nick Milner-Gulland (1940-2017)*

As time went on you grafted both your hearts
Onto the little grange at Valojoulx
And for a few brief weeks in every year
He put on hold enriching others' lives
And let the sights and sounds of rural France
Enrich his own,
Refuel the restless engine of his mind
And offer up those small indulgences
That daily life precludes.

One was the birds: he loved to watch
(With something pale and gently chilled at hand)
The buzzards floating down towards the valley
Low over the house, then working the fields beyond,
Searching for prey.

So, after the tributes and memorials
You bravely made a pilgrimage to France
To exorcise the spirits that cried out:
"This was a place for both of you, or none!"
And seated on the terrace late that day
You spied a dark speck puncturing the sky,
An apparition growing from the south,
No flock, but just one solitary bird,
A golden buzzard circling the house,
Throwing out its plaintive mew in greeting,
Then off and away, soaring ever higher
Until it was a tiny speck again,
Silhouetted in the sinking sun.

And do you believe that proud and lovely bird,
Among the deep mysteries of the far-beyond,
Was somehow linked to him who shared your life,
A cosmic envoy, urging strength and faith
And love undying?

# Cowslips At Didling

West of Midhurst the Downs, their backs to the sea,
Plunge into the Rother,
The steep green slopes dissolving into ridges
Like paws clawing at the Weald
Where City bankers play at gentle farming,
But also, all those centuries ago,
Where poor communities built simple churches,
So modest and remote
That antiquarians of more recent times
Passed them by
For grander icons of the Gothic idiom.

These Shepherds' churches,
Little more than consecrated barns,
Bear witness in their scale and truthfulness
To something lasting and profound.

Unearth the one at Didling, plain and whitewashed,
A single, undelineated space
Lit by cast-iron candelabra whose flickering lights
Pick out the ancient pews, rough-hewn, original,
The Saxon font and simple lancet windows.

You reach it by a track
That leads off from a narrow, winding,
Semi-tarmac-ed road,
Revealed at last behind its citadel of
Huge and venerable trees,
Beech and lime and statutory yew
That may pre-date the very church itself,
Fenced off from flocks of bleating lambs
In the fields around.

And wait! Not all those golden smudges in the churchyard
Are primroses and dandelions: some are cowslips
Sprinkled under the leaning tombstones,
Rare and magic in the mid-May sun.

Behind the wire bird-gate at the porch
There hangs a framed chart listing the Didling Vicars
From twelve fourteen up to the present day,
Next to which, in laborious manuscript,
An invitation to the world at large
To attend a service in this house of God
'At Eastertide and Christmas,
Details to be posted in the porch.'

## FOR ART'S SAKE

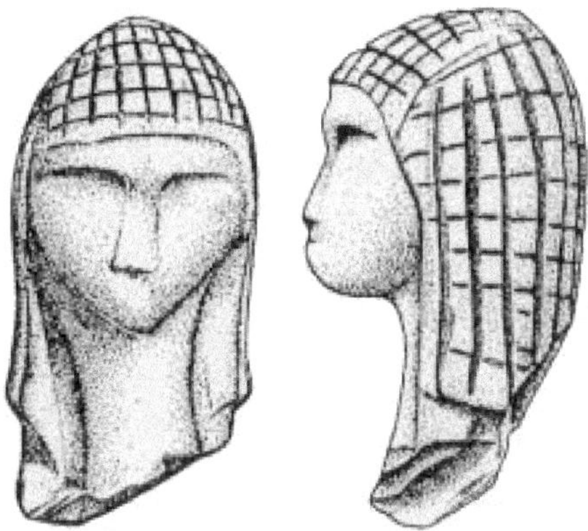

*La Dame de Brassempouy is a fragmentary ivory figurine found in the cave of Brassempouy, France in 1892. About 25,000 years old she is one of the earliest known representations of a human face.*

Here's Civilisation's savant, Simon Schama,
Unfolding his artistic panorama,
Erudition, super-synthesis,
Rivalling Clark's great precedent to his.

He moulds his argument in many shapes
To show our kind are more than trousered apes;
Admitting none can truly say what art is
But, nothing venture, offers us for starters

Pre-Art Neanderthals, who never felt a
Need for anything but food and shelter,
So through the History Man's reflecting lens
We view the dawn of Homo Sapiens

And each exhibit caught in Schama's noose,
Like patterned surfaces *that had no use*,
And then move forward forty thousand years
To reach a cave in Portugal that bears

Images of bison done in colour,
Than when they were created hardly duller,
To fascinate all those who would come later
Far beyond the life of their creator,

A language that all other species lack
In archetypal yellow, red and black,
Saliva mixed with powder into paint,
Preserved in time like relics of a saint,

Then finally *La Dame de Brassempouy*
Carved from mammoth's tusk, this effigy,
The oldest sculptured image that we know,
From twenty-five millennia ago,

Triangular face with forehead, nose and brows
Shaped in relief our wonder to arouse:
Modern history's poignant curtain-raiser
And pretty, even to to-day's appraiser!

# 2020 MELTDOWN

Where were the cars and the talk in the bars
In the silence that no-one foresaw?
Was it an enemy envoy from Mars
Who declared inter-planetary war?

One day the lark offered peace from the ark
Its song so familiar and bold;
The next brought the murderous virus's bark
As the planet was frozen on hold.

This is no joke, but a time to invoke,
Though fragile, the nation's defiance,
But the Reaper assumes his invisible cloak,
Enforcing his terms for compliance.

Now empty the churches, society lurches,
The virus is taking its toll;
Wherever it lurks its fell purpose besmirches,
It kidnaps both body and soul.

Strong men they crieth, communities dieth,
No mercy for rich or for poor;
The virus a David, the planet Goliath,
Our weapons effective no more.

In vain exorcism, this deft organism
Pollutes with its poison the earth;
It fractures consensus to substitute schism,
Respects neither merit nor birth.

It's out of our orbit, we cannot absorb it,
It gnaws at our national pride;
How to react to an outcome so morbid? -
Forty-eight thousand have died.

All we can bet, and it's not over yet,
Is that naught short of total extinction
Will pose to us all a more nightmarish threat,
A more terrible mark of distinction.

# INDEX TO TITLES